THIS BOOK BELONGS TO

_____

_____

START DATE _____ / _____ / _____

HE READS TRUTH

EXECUTIVE

**FOUNDER /
CHIEF EXECUTIVE OFFICER**
Raechel Myers

**CO-FOUNDER /
CHIEF CONTENT OFFICER**
Amanda Bible Williams

CHIEF OPERATING OFFICER
Ryan Myers

EXECUTIVE ASSISTANT
Sarah Andereck

EDITORIAL

CONTENT DIRECTOR
John Greco, MDiv

MANAGING EDITOR
Jessica Lamb

CONTENT EDITOR
Kara Gause

ASSOCIATE EDITORS
Bailey Gillespie
Ellen Taylor

CREATIVE

CREATIVE DIRECTOR
Jeremy Mitchell

LEAD DESIGNER
Kelsea Allen

DESIGNERS
Abbey Benson
Davis DeLisi
Annie Glover

MARKETING

MARKETING DIRECTOR
Hannah Warren

MARKETING MANAGER
Katie Pierce

SOCIAL MEDIA MANAGER
Ansley Rushing

COMMUNITY SUPPORT SPECIALIST
Margot Williams

SHIPPING & LOGISTICS

LOGISTICS MANAGER
Lauren Gloyne

SHIPPING MANAGER
Sydney Bess

CUSTOMER SUPPORT SPECIALIST
Katy McKnight

FULFILLMENT SPECIALISTS
Abigail Achord
Cait Baggerman
Kamiren Passavanti

SUBSCRIPTION INQUIRIES
orders@hereadstruth.com

CONTRIBUTOR

ARTIST
Carrie Moradi (42, 76, 100, 138)

COLOPHON

This book was printed offset in Nashville, Tennessee, on 60# Lynx Opaque Text under the direction of He Reads Truth. The cover is 100# Neenah Royal Sundance White Felt.

COPYRIGHT

© 2020 by He Reads Truth, LLC
All rights reserved.

ISBN 978-1-952670-00-8

1 2 3 4 5 6 7 8 9 10

No part of this publication may be reproduced, distributed, or transmitted in any form or by any means, including photocopying, recording, or other electronic or mechanical methods, without the prior written permission of He Reads Truth, LLC, except in the case of brief quotations embodied in critical reviews and certain other noncommercial uses permitted by copyright law.

All Scripture is taken from the Christian Standard Bible®. Copyright © 2020 by Holman Bible Publishers. Used by permission. Christian Standard Bible® and CSB® are federally registered trademarks of Holman Bible Publishers.

Research support provided by Logos Bible Software™. Learn more at logos.com.

HEREADSTRUTH.COM @HEREADSTRUTH Download the He Reads Truth app, available for iOS and Android.

THE PRESENCE OF GOD

HE READS TRUTH

KEY VERSE
PSALM 73:28

BUT AS FOR ME, GOD'S PRESENCE IS MY GOOD. I HAVE MADE THE LORD GOD MY REFUGE, SO I CAN TELL ABOUT ALL YOU DO.

WELCOME LETTER

When we look for the theme of God's presence in Scripture, we start to find it on every page. We see God described in awe-inspiring ways. He is enthroned on high (Ps 113:4-6). He fills the heavens and the earth. There is nowhere we can go where He doesn't see us (Ps 139; Jr 23:24).

But Scripture has so much more to say about God's presence. In passage after passage, we're told that God also desires to be specifically, relationally present with His people. Authors and Bible scholars J. Scott Duvall and J. Daniel Hayes even suggest this is the central theme of the entire Bible.

God heard every time the enslaved Israelites cried out against the injustice they suffered in Egypt (Ex 3:9), and He showed up in a visible pillar of cloud and fire to lead them on their journey out of captivity (Ex 13:20-22).

God is before all things and holds all things together (Col 1:17), and He intercedes for us in wordless groans when, in our weakness, we don't know the words to pray (Rm 8:26-27).

God can't be contained in any house built by human hands (1Kg 8:27; Ac 17:24), yet He walked off the dusty roads of Judea and into the homes of sinners, tax collectors, drunkards, and fisherman to eat and drink with them (Mt 24:49; Lk 10:38-42; 19:1-10).

This book is an invitation to dig into what Scripture has to say about God's presence. One of our favorite features is found on pages 12-17: prompts for practicing the presence of God. If you struggle to quiet the noise around and inside you, we encourage you to plan ahead to try some of these practices and reflect on your experience.

As you'll discover in this reading plan, we were created for this kind of relationship with God—to live in His presence, experience His goodness, and enjoy Him all the days of our lives. God has always drawn near to His people, and even now, He invites us to draw near to Him

Read on.

THE HE READS TRUTH TEAM

Each He Reads Truth resource is thoughtfully and artfully designed to highlight the beauty, goodness, and truth of Scripture in a way that reflects the themes of each curated reading plan.

The tissue paper artwork from artist Carrie Moradi found throughout the book is inspired by landscapes and architecture. This artwork reminds us of places where God's presence is found in Scripture: natural elements like mountains, dense clouds, and rushing water, as well as divinely inspired, man-made elements like the tabernacle and the temple.

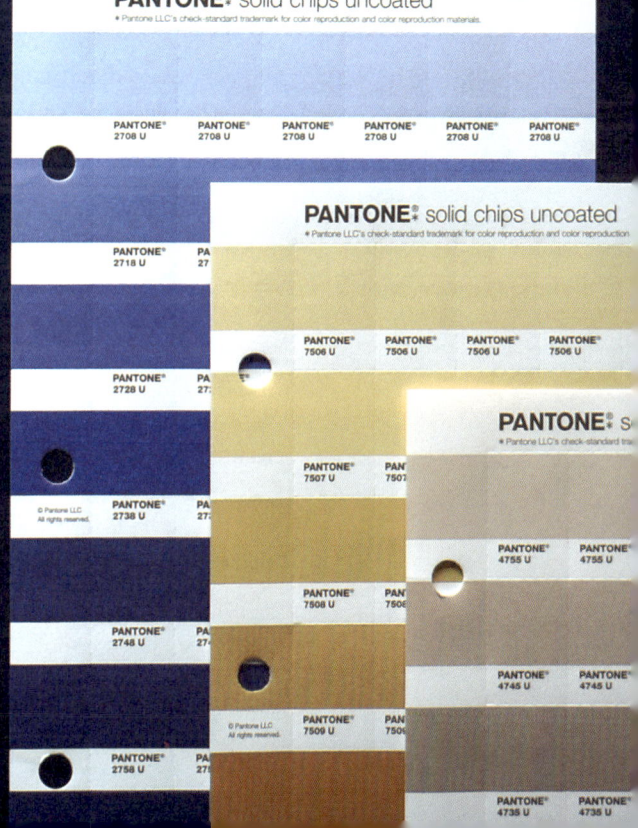

The color palette was inspired by Ezekiel 10:1, which describes the throne of God as having "the appearance of lapis lazuli." The rich navy alludes to this lapis lazuli stone, while the gold reminds us of the gift of God's presence.

HOW TO USE THIS BOOK

Each book in the He Reads Truth Legacy Series™ provides space to read and study Scripture, make notes, and record prayers. As you build your library, you will have a record of your Bible-reading journey to reference and pass down.

SCRIPTURE READING

Designed for a Monday start, this Legacy Book presents daily readings on the presence of God.

JOURNALING SPACE

Each section features space for notes and guided prompts to help you reflect on God's presence.

GRACE DAY

Use Saturdays to catch up on your reading, pray, and rest in the presence of the Lord.

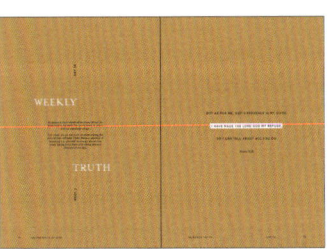

WEEKLY TRUTH

Sundays are set aside for Scripture memorization.

EXTRAS

This book features additional tools to help you gain a deeper understanding of the text.

Devotionals corresponding to each daily reading can be found in **The Presence of God** reading plan at HeReadsTruth.com or on the He Reads Truth app.

TABLE OF CONTENTS

1 — GOD IS WITH US

Extra	Practicing the Presence of God	12
Introduction	God Is with Us	18
DAY 1	Our Ever-Present God	20
Extra	Attributes of God	23
DAY 2	We Are Welcomed into God's Presence	26
DAY 3	God's Presence Strengthens Us	30
Hymn	I Need Thee Every Hour	34
DAY 4	God Gives Us Peace and Rest	36
DAY 5	Remembering God's Presence	38
DAY 6	Grace Day	43
DAY 7	Weekly Truth	44
Response	God Is with Us	46

2 — GOD'S DWELLING PLACE

Introduction	God's Dwelling Place	48
DAY 8	Life with God in the Garden	50
DAY 9	God Leads His People into His Presence	54
Extra	Mountains of God	58
DAY 10	God's Presence Transforms His People	62
DAY 11	God Dwells Among His People in the Tabernacle	66
DAY 12	God's Presence Fills the Temple	70
DAY 13	Grace Day	77
DAY 14	Weekly Truth	78
DAY 15	God's Presence Leaves the Temple	80

DAY 16	One Greater Than the Temple	84
DAY 17	The Pouring Out of God's Spirit	88
Extra	Sacred Space	94
DAY 18	The Temple of the Living God	96
DAY 19	Life with God in the Garden City	98
DAY 20	Grace Day	101
DAY 21	Weekly Truth	102
Response	God's Dwelling Place	104

3 — THE PROMISE OF GOD'S PRESENCE

Introduction	The Promise of God's Presence	106
DAY 22	God Promises His Presence	108
DAY 23	God's Presence Equips Us	112
DAY 24	Walking in God's Presence	116
Extra	Psalms, Worship, and the Presence of God	120
DAY 25	God's Presence Is with Us Always	130
DAY 26	Eternity in God's Presence	134
DAY 27	Grace Day	139
DAY 28	Weekly Truth	140
Response	The Promise of God's Presence	142
Extra	For the Record	156

PRACTICING *the* PRESENCE *of* GOD

God promises never to leave us. The Holy Spirit is present in all believers, and Jesus told us He would be with us always (Mt 28:20; Jn 14:16–17). Throughout this study, set aside time to practice the presence of God using the tips and reminders on the following pages as a guide. You'll find space to reflect on your experience at the end of each section, as well as extra response sheets at the back of this book for personal use.

MAKE INTENTIONAL TIME AND SPACE

Though we often experience the presence of God with other believers at church or at other corporate gatherings, we also need to spend one-on-one time with Him. Even Jesus withdrew to be with His Father (Mt 14:13; Lk 22:39–41). When we create space and margin for Him in our lives, we may be surprised by how He fills it.

Choose a time in advance and set an appointment on your calendar. Try carving out fifteen minutes in the morning or before you go to bed, or finding a quiet spot over your lunch break—whatever works best for you.

Find a place—in your home, your car, or outdoors—where you are, ideally, by yourself.

Create a peaceful setting, one free of distraction—it doesn't have to be perfect. Consider closing your eyes to help you focus.

If you do become distracted, don't worry. Your mind's inner chatter might be loud when you first try to sit quietly, but keep practicing.

MEDITATE ON GOD'S WORD

Meditating on God's Word means taking time to slowly read and think about Scripture and what it tells us about who God is (Jos 1:8; Ps 1:1–3; 19:14; Php 4:8). When we make Scripture an ongoing part of everyday life, it will transform our hearts and minds.

Through His Word, God shapes us and equips us for the good works He has prepared in advance for us to do (Jn 15:2, 7; Eph 2:10).

Many Christians find praying the words of Scripture to be a powerful experience, especially in times of grief (Ps 56:4).

Memorizing individual verses and longer passages helps us internalize what we have read. When we memorize Scripture, we are better prepared for the trials of the Christian life (Mt 4:1–11). To start, consider memorizing the Weekly Truth passage from this study.

Name God's character traits that stand out from your Scripture reading, and spend time reflecting on them.

PRAY

Ask God to meet with you, speak to you, and show you things in new ways. You might imagine that you're walking and talking with a good friend who's by your side. In reality, God is with us always, so we can talk with Him all day long. When we talk to God, we can be confident that He hears and answers us (Jr 29:12–13; 1 Jn 5:14).

Thank God for who He is and how He has provided for you (Ps 103:1-2).

Pray for the needs of the greater Church and the world (Mt 6:9-13). Pray for your own personal needs (Mk 10:51).

Pray using the Lord's Prayer as a guide (Mt 6:9-13). Consider pausing after each phrase, allowing it to form your conversation with God.

As the apostle Paul said, we are to "pray constantly" (1Th 5:17). Think of ways you can remind yourself to pause and pray throughout the day, like setting an alert on your phone or placing a verse where you'll see it often.

Pray through the psalms found on pages 120-129 as a means of seeking, celebrating, lamenting, and resting in God's presence.

Choose to read a prayer, blessing, or poem about God that someone else has written as a guide.

Spend time not only talking to God, but listening as well. Jesus said that His sheep know His voice (Jn 10:4). Remember, if listening to God in this way is new for you, it may be hard to be silent at first. Don't be discouraged. It will get easier with time.

WORSHIP

Being in God's presence doesn't always look like sitting still and being quiet. There are many different ways to embrace God's presence through worship.

Walk, dance, sing, or play a musical instrument (2Sm 6:14; Ps 149:3).

Engage in corporate worship with your local church (Ac 2:42–45).

Participate in the Lord's Supper with your local church (1Co 11:23–26).

Serve the people around you (Mt 25:35–40).

Praise God for His nearness or lament that He doesn't feel as near as you would like (Ps 10; 34).

CONFESS

The more time we spend with Jesus, the more our own sin, indifference, and insecurities come to the surface as the Holy Spirit continues to make us more like Him (2Co 3:18; Jms 4:8).

Ask the Holy Spirit to bring sin to your attention. Confess it and receive Christ's forgiveness.

Read assurances of pardon, grace, and forgiveness from Scripture, such as Ephesians 1:7–8. As you read, ask yourself, "Do I believe this is true?"

1

GOD IS WITH US

> See, the virgin will become pregnant and give birth to a son, and they will name him Immanuel, which is translated "God is with us."
>
> MATTHEW 1:23

God is present everywhere. He is before all things, He created all things, He is above all things, and He holds all things together. But our Creator God is also personally, intimately involved with His creation and His people. He created us to live in communion with Him. In His presence, we find joy and abundant life.

DAY 1

OUR EVER-PRESENT GOD

God is not only universally present above and beyond creation; He is also personally present, dwelling with His people.

PSALM 139:1-10

THE ALL-KNOWING, EVER-PRESENT GOD

For the choir director. A psalm of David.

¹ Lord, you have searched me and known me.
² You know when I sit down and when I stand up;
you understand my thoughts from far away.
³ You observe my travels and my rest;
you are aware of all my ways.
⁴ Before a word is on my tongue,
you know all about it, Lord.
⁵ You have encircled me;
you have placed your hand on me.
⁶ This wondrous knowledge is beyond me.
It is lofty; I am unable to reach it.

⁷ Where can I go to escape your Spirit?
Where can I flee from your presence?
⁸ If I go up to heaven, you are there;
if I make my bed in Sheol, you are there.
⁹ If I fly on the wings of the dawn
or settle at the western limits,
¹⁰ even there your hand will lead me;
your right hand will hold on to me.

EXODUS 33:16

How will it be known that I and your people have found favor with you unless you go with us? I and your people will be distinguished by this from all the other people on the face of the earth.

JEREMIAH 23:23-24

²³ "Am I a God who is only near"—this is the Lord's declaration—"and not a God who is far away? ²⁴ Can a person hide in secret places where I cannot see him?" —the Lord's declaration. "Do I not fill the heavens and the earth?" —the Lord's declaration.

NOTES

ISAIAH 66:1-2

[1] This is what the LORD says:

> Heaven is my throne,
> and earth is my footstool.
> Where could you possibly build a house for me?
> And where would my resting place be?
> [2] My hand made all these things,
> and so they all came into being.
>   This is the LORD's declaration.
> I will look favorably on this kind of person:
> one who is humble, submissive in spirit,
> and trembles at my word.

MATTHEW 1:20-23

[20] But after he had considered these things, an angel of the Lord appeared to him in a dream, saying, "Joseph, son of David, don't be afraid to take Mary as your wife, because what has been conceived in her is from the Holy Spirit. [21] She will give birth to a son, and you are to name him Jesus, because he will save his people from their sins."

[22] Now all this took place to fulfill what was spoken by the Lord through the prophet:

> [23] See, the virgin will become pregnant
> and give birth to a son,
> and they will name him Immanuel,

which is translated "God is with us."

JOHN 1:29-34

[29] The next day John saw Jesus coming toward him and said, "Look, the Lamb of God, who takes away the sin of the world! [30] This is the one I told you about: 'After me comes a man who ranks ahead of me, because he existed before me.' [31] I didn't know him, but I came baptizing with water so that he might be revealed to Israel." [32] And John testified, "I saw the Spirit descending from heaven like a dove, and he rested on him. [33] I didn't know him, but he who sent me to baptize with water told me, 'The one you see the Spirit descending and resting on—he is the one who baptizes with the Holy Spirit.' [34] I have seen and testified that this is the Son of God."

ATTRIBUTES OF GOD

Below, we've defined a few terms often used when talking about the presence of God.

1 TRANSCENDENCE

God is beyond all human comprehension, including the human limitations of space and time. God is distinct from His creation because He created it and rules over it. God is "above" creation in the sense that He is greater than and independent of creation.

2 IMMANENCE

He continues to be involved in creation, which depends on Him for its existence and functioning. He also interacts within creation, specifically through revealing Himself in Jesus and the Holy Spirit.

3 OMNIPRESENCE

There is no escaping God's presence. He sees everything and is everywhere, all the time.

4 THE MANIFEST PRESENCE OF GOD

Believers experience God's presence in the material world. Though God is omnipresent, Scripture also describes instances where God's presence becomes visible or potent in unique ways, like during miracles, worship, concentrated gatherings of believers, or in Christ's ministry on earth.

NOTES

ACTS 17:22-29

²² Paul stood in the middle of the Areopagus and said: "People of Athens! I see that you are extremely religious in every respect. ²³ For as I was passing through and observing the objects of your worship, I even found an altar on which was inscribed: 'To an Unknown God.' Therefore, what you worship in ignorance, this I proclaim to you. ²⁴ The God who made the world and everything in it—he is Lord of heaven and earth—does not live in shrines made by hands. ²⁵ Neither is he served by human hands, as though he needed anything, since he himself gives everyone life and breath and all things. ²⁶ From one man he has made every nationality to live over the whole earth and has determined their appointed times and the boundaries of where they live. ²⁷ He did this so that they might seek God, and perhaps they might reach out and find him, though he is not far from each one of us. ²⁸ For in him we live and move and have our being, as even some of your own poets have said, 'For we are also his offspring.' ²⁹ Since we are God's offspring then, we shouldn't think that the divine nature is like gold or silver or stone, an image fashioned by human art and imagination."

COLOSSIANS 1:16-20

¹⁶ For everything was created by him,
in heaven and on earth,
the visible and the invisible,
whether thrones or dominions
or rulers or authorities—
all things have been created through him and for him.
¹⁷ He is before all things,
and by him all things hold together.
¹⁸ He is also the head of the body, the church;
he is the beginning,
the firstborn from the dead,
so that he might come to have
first place in everything.
¹⁹ For God was pleased to have
all his fullness dwell in him,
²⁰ and through him to reconcile
everything to himself,
whether things on earth or things in heaven,
by making peace
through his blood, shed on the cross.

NOTES

DATE

DAY 2

WE ARE WELCOMED INTO GOD'S PRESENCE

Our holy God, through His grace and provision, welcomes imperfect people into His presence.

LEVITICUS 11:45

"For I am the Lord, who brought you up from the land of Egypt to be your God, so you must be holy because I am holy."

PSALM 27:4

I have asked one thing from the Lord;
it is what I desire:
to dwell in the house of the Lord
all the days of my life,
gazing on the beauty of the Lord
and seeking him in his temple.

ISAIAH 6:1–7

ISAIAH'S CALL AND MISSION

¹ In the year that King Uzziah died, I saw the Lord seated on a high and lofty throne, and the hem of his robe filled the temple. ² Seraphim were standing above him; they each had six wings: with two they covered their faces, with two they covered their feet, and with two they flew. ³ And one called to another:

> Holy, holy, holy is the Lord of Armies;
> his glory fills the whole earth.

⁴ The foundations of the doorways shook at the sound of their voices, and the temple was filled with smoke.

⁵ Then I said:

> Woe is me for I am ruined
> because I am a man of unclean lips
> and live among a people of unclean lips,
> and because my eyes have seen the King,
> the Lord of Armies.

⁶ Then one of the seraphim flew to me, and in his hand was a glowing coal that he had taken from the altar with tongs. ⁷ He touched my mouth with it and said:

NOTES

> Now that this has touched your lips,
> your iniquity is removed
> and your sin is atoned for.

EPHESIANS 2:13–18

¹³ But now in Christ Jesus, you who were far away have been brought near by the blood of Christ. ¹⁴ For he is our peace, who made both groups one and tore down the dividing wall of hostility. In his flesh, ¹⁵ he made of no effect the law consisting of commands and expressed in regulations, so that he might create in himself one new man from the two, resulting in peace. ¹⁶ He did this so that he might reconcile both to God in one body through the cross by which he put the hostility to death. ¹⁷ He came and proclaimed the good news of peace to you who were far away and peace to those who were near. ¹⁸ For through him we both have access in one Spirit to the Father.

HEBREWS 4:16

> Therefore, let us approach the throne of grace with boldness, so that we may receive mercy and find grace to help us in time of need.

JUDE 24–25

²⁴ Now to him who is able to protect you from stumbling and to make you stand in the presence of his glory, without blemish and with great joy, ²⁵ to the only God our Savior, through Jesus Christ our Lord, be glory, majesty, power, and authority before all time, now and forever. Amen.

REVELATION 4

THE THRONE ROOM OF HEAVEN

¹ After this I looked, and there in heaven was an open door. The first voice that I had heard speaking to me like a trumpet said, "Come up here, and I will show you what must take place after this."

² Immediately I was in the Spirit, and there was a throne in heaven and someone was seated on it. ³ The one seated there had the appearance of jasper and carnelian stone. A rainbow that had the appearance of an emerald surrounded the throne.

⁴ Around the throne were twenty-four thrones, and on the thrones sat twenty-four elders dressed in white clothes, with golden crowns on their heads.

⁵ Flashes of lightning and rumblings and peals of thunder came from the throne. Seven fiery torches were burning before the throne, which are the seven spirits of God. ⁶ Something like a sea of glass, similar to crystal, was also before the throne.

Four living creatures covered with eyes in front and in back were around the throne on each side. ⁷ The first living creature was like a lion; the second living creature was like an ox; the third living creature had a face like a man; and the fourth living creature was like a flying eagle. ⁸ Each of the four living creatures had six wings; they were covered with eyes around and inside. Day and night they never stop, saying,

> Holy, holy, holy,
> Lord God, the Almighty,
> who was, who is, and who is to come.

⁹ Whenever the living creatures give glory, honor, and thanks to the one seated on the throne, the one who lives forever and ever, ¹⁰ the twenty-four elders fall down before the one seated on the throne and worship the one who lives forever and ever. They cast their crowns before the throne and say,

> ¹¹ Our Lord and God,
> you are worthy to receive
> glory and honor and power,
> because you have created all things,
> and by your will
> they exist and were created.

NOTES

DAY 3

GOD'S PRESENCE STRENGTHENS US

We can find courage and hope to endure all things because the powerful presence of our God goes with us.

DEUTERONOMY 31:6–8

⁶ "Be strong and courageous; don't be terrified or afraid of them. For the Lord your God is the one who will go with you; he will not leave you or abandon you."

⁷ Moses then summoned Joshua and said to him in the sight of all Israel, "Be strong and courageous, for you will go with this people into the land the Lord swore to give to their ancestors. You will enable them to take possession of it. ⁸ The Lord is the one who will go before you. He will be with you; he will not leave you or abandon you. Do not be afraid or discouraged."

PSALM 46

GOD OUR REFUGE

For the choir director. A song of the sons of Korah. According to Alamoth.

¹ God is our refuge and strength,
a helper who is always found
in times of trouble.
² Therefore we will not be afraid,
though the earth trembles
and the mountains topple
into the depths of the seas,
³ though its water roars and foams
and the mountains quake with its turmoil.   *Selah*

⁴ There is a river—
its streams delight the city of God,
the holy dwelling place of the Most High.
⁵ God is within her; she will not be toppled.
God will help her when the morning dawns.
⁶ Nations rage, kingdoms topple;
the earth melts when he lifts his voice.
⁷ The Lord of Armies is with us;
the God of Jacob is our stronghold.   *Selah*

⁸ Come, see the works of the Lord,
who brings devastation on the earth.
⁹ He makes wars cease throughout the earth.

NOTES

He shatters bows and cuts spears to pieces;
he sets wagons ablaze.
[10] "Stop fighting, and know that I am God,
exalted among the nations, exalted on the earth."
[11] The Lord of Armies is with us;
the God of Jacob is our stronghold.   *Selah*

ZEPHANIAH 3:17

"The Lord your God is among you,
a warrior who saves.
He will rejoice over you with gladness.
He will be quiet in his love.
He will delight in you with singing."

ISAIAH 40:9-11

[9] Zion, herald of good news,
go up on a high mountain.
Jerusalem, herald of good news,
raise your voice loudly.
Raise it, do not be afraid!
Say to the cities of Judah,
"Here is your God!"
[10] See, the Lord God comes with strength,
and his power establishes his rule.
His wages are with him,
and his reward accompanies him.
[11] He protects his flock like a shepherd;
he gathers the lambs in his arms
and carries them in the fold of his garment.
He gently leads those that are nursing.

ISAIAH 41:10

"Do not fear, for I am with you;
do not be afraid, for I am your God.
I will strengthen you; I will help you;
I will hold on to you with my righteous right hand."

2 TIMOTHY 4:16–18

¹⁶ At my first defense, no one stood by me, but everyone deserted me. May it not be counted against them. ¹⁷ But the Lord stood with me and strengthened me, so that I might fully preach the word and all the Gentiles might hear it. So I was rescued from the lion's mouth.

¹⁸ The Lord will rescue me from every evil work and will bring me safely into his heavenly kingdom.

To him be the glory forever and ever! Amen.

HYMN

I NEED THEE EVERY HOUR

I need Thee ev'ry hour,
most gracious Lord;
No tender voice like Thine
can peace afford.

I need Thee, O I need Thee;
every hour I need Thee!
O bless me now, my Savior,
I come to Thee.

I need Thee ev'ry hour,
stay Thou nearby;
Temptations lose their pow'r
when Thou art nigh.

I need Thee ev'ry hour,
in joy or pain;
Come quickly and abide,
or life is vain.

I need Thee ev'ry hour,
teach me Thy will;
Thy promises so rich
in me fulfill.

I need Thee ev'ry hour,
most Holy One;
O make me Thine indeed,
Thou blessed Son.

Words: Annie S. Hawks
Music: Robert Lowry

DAY 4

GOD GIVES US PEACE AND REST

When we remember God's presence goes with us and before us, we can find comfort in any circumstance.

EXODUS 33:12-17

THE LORD'S GLORY

¹² Moses said to the Lord, "Look, you have told me, 'Lead this people up,' but you have not let me know whom you will send with me. You said, 'I know you by name, and you have also found favor with me.' ¹³ Now if I have indeed found favor with you, please teach me your ways, and I will know you, so that I may find favor with you. Now consider that this nation is your people."

¹⁴ And he replied, "My presence will go with you, and I will give you rest."

¹⁵ "If your presence does not go," Moses responded to him, "don't make us go up from here. ¹⁶ How will it be known that I and your people have found favor with you unless you go with us? I and your people will be distinguished by this from all the other people on the face of the earth."

¹⁷ The Lord answered Moses, "I will do this very thing you have asked, for you have found favor with me, and I know you by name."

NUMBERS 6:22-27

THE PRIESTLY BLESSING

²² The Lord spoke to Moses: ²³ "Tell Aaron and his sons, 'This is how you are to bless the Israelites. You should say to them,

> ²⁴ "May the Lord bless you and protect you;
> ²⁵ may the Lord make his face shine on you
> and be gracious to you;
> ²⁶ may the Lord look with favor on you
> and give you peace."'

²⁷ In this way they will pronounce my name over the Israelites, and I will bless them."

PSALM 16:11

You reveal the path of life to me;
in your presence is abundant joy;
at your right hand are eternal pleasures.

PSALM 23

THE GOOD SHEPHERD

A psalm of David.

¹ The Lord is my shepherd;
I have what I need.
² He lets me lie down in green pastures;
he leads me beside quiet waters.
³ He renews my life;
he leads me along the right paths
for his name's sake.
⁴ Even when I go through the darkest valley,
I fear no danger,
for you are with me;
your rod and your staff—they comfort me.

⁵ You prepare a table before me
in the presence of my enemies;
you anoint my head with oil;
my cup overflows.
⁶ Only goodness and faithful love will pursue me
all the days of my life,
and I will dwell in the house of the Lord
as long as I live.

ROMANS 15:13

Now may the God of hope fill you with all joy and peace as you believe so that you may overflow with hope by the power of the Holy Spirit.

2 THESSALONIANS 3:16

May the Lord of peace himself give you peace always in every way. The Lord be with all of you.

DAY 5

REMEMBERING GOD'S PRESENCE

As we focus our hearts and minds on Him, we become more aware of our ever-present God.

DEUTERONOMY 4:29-31

²⁹ But from there, you will search for the LORD your God, and you will find him when you seek him with all your heart and all your soul.

³⁰ When you are in distress and all these things have happened to you, in the future you will return to the LORD your God and obey him. ³¹ He will not leave you, destroy you, or forget the covenant with your fathers that he swore to them by oath, because the LORD your God is a compassionate God.

1 CHRONICLES 16:7-36

DAVID'S PSALM OF THANKSGIVING

⁷ On that day David decreed for the first time that thanks be given to the LORD by Asaph and his relatives:

⁸ Give thanks to the LORD; call on his name;
proclaim his deeds among the peoples.
⁹ Sing to him; sing praise to him;
tell about all his wondrous works!
¹⁰ Boast in his holy name;
let the hearts of those who seek the LORD rejoice.
¹¹ Seek the LORD and his strength;
seek his face always.
¹² Remember the wondrous works he has done,
his wonders, and the judgments he has pronounced,
¹³ you offspring of Israel his servant,
Jacob's descendants—his chosen ones.

¹⁴ He is the LORD our God;
his judgments govern the whole earth.
¹⁵ Remember his covenant forever—
the promise he ordained for a thousand generations,
¹⁶ the covenant he made with Abraham,
swore to Isaac,
¹⁷ and confirmed to Jacob as a decree,
and to Israel as a permanent covenant:

NOTES

[18] "I will give the land of Canaan to you
as your inherited portion."

[19] When they were few in number,
very few indeed, and resident aliens in Canaan
[20] wandering from nation to nation
and from one kingdom to another,
[21] he allowed no one to oppress them;
he rebuked kings on their behalf:
[22] "Do not touch my anointed ones
or harm my prophets."

[23] Let the whole earth sing to the Lord.
Proclaim his salvation from day to day.
[24] Declare his glory among the nations,
his wondrous works among all peoples.

[25] For the Lord is great and highly praised;
he is feared above all gods.
[26] For all the gods of the peoples are worthless idols,
but the Lord made the heavens.
[27] Splendor and majesty are before him;
strength and joy are in his place.
[28] Ascribe to the Lord, families of the peoples,
ascribe to the Lord glory and strength.
[29] Ascribe to the Lord the glory of his name;
bring an offering and come before him.
Worship the Lord in the splendor of his holiness;
[30] let the whole earth tremble before him.
The world is firmly established;
it cannot be shaken.
[31] Let the heavens be glad and the earth rejoice,
and let them say among the nations, "The Lord reigns!"
[32] Let the sea and all that fills it resound;
let the fields and everything in them exult.
[33] Then the trees of the forest will shout for joy before the Lord,
for he is coming to judge the earth.

[34] Give thanks to the Lord, for he is good;
his faithful love endures forever.

³⁵ And say, "Save us, God of our salvation;
gather us and rescue us from the nations
so that we may give thanks to your holy name
and rejoice in your praise.
³⁶ Blessed be the LORD God of Israel
from everlasting to everlasting."

Then all the people said, "Amen" and "Praise the LORD."

PSALM 73:28

But as for me, God's presence is my good.
I have made the Lord GOD my refuge,
so I can tell about all you do.

COLOSSIANS 3:14-17

¹⁴ Above all, put on love, which is the perfect bond of unity. ¹⁵ And let the peace of Christ, to which you were also called in one body, rule your hearts. And be thankful. ¹⁶ Let the word of Christ dwell richly among you, in all wisdom teaching and admonishing one another through psalms, hymns, and spiritual songs, singing to God with gratitude in your hearts. ¹⁷ And whatever you do, in word or in deed, do everything in the name of the Lord Jesus, giving thanks to God the Father through him.

GRACE DAY

Take this day to catch up on your reading,
pray, and rest in the presence of the Lord.

LORD, you have searched me
and known me. You know
when I sit down and when I
stand up; you understand my
thoughts from far away.

PSALM 139:1-2

DAY 6

DAY 7

WEEKLY

Scripture is God-breathed and true. When we memorize it, we carry the good news of Jesus with us wherever we go.

During this reading plan, we will memorize Psalm 73:28. Ask a friend to memorize this verse with you over the next few weeks, and make it a priority to check in with one another as you commit the verse to memory. This week, focus on memorizing the first line.

TRUTH

WEEK 1

BUT AS FOR ME, GOD'S PRESENCE IS MY GOOD.

I HAVE MADE THE LORD GOD MY REFUGE,

SO I CAN TELL ABOUT ALL YOU DO.

Psalm 73:28

SECTION 1

"You need not cry very loud; He is nearer to us than we are aware of."

BROTHER LAWRENCE

In response to what you've read and learned in Section 1 about the presence of God, take time to focus on His presence using one or more of the practices listed here. For tips and reminders about each one, refer back to pages 12-17. Use the space provided to journal about or reflect on your experience.

Make intentional time and space.
Meditate on God's Word.
Pray.
Worship.
Confess.

Additional response sheets are included on pages 146-153.

GOD IS WITH US

RESPONSE

DATE

2

GOD'S DWELLING PLACE

> Look, God's dwelling is with humanity, and he will live with them. They will be his peoples, and God himself will be with them and will be their God.
>
> REVELATION 21:3

The Bible tells the story of how our relational, holy God comes to dwell with His people. We were created for life in God's presence. But in our sin, we could not come close to Him. So He came to us—on mountains and in temples, in the person of Jesus Christ, and through the Holy Spirit.

DAY 8

LIFE WITH GOD IN THE GARDEN

God created us to live and serve in His presence, but our sin made us unfit for life in the garden.

GENESIS 2:7-9, 15-22

7 Then the Lord God formed the man out of the dust from the ground and breathed the breath of life into his nostrils, and the man became a living being.

8 The Lord God planted a garden in Eden, in the east, and there he placed the man he had formed. 9 The Lord God caused to grow out of the ground every tree pleasing in appearance and good for food, including the tree of life in the middle of the garden, as well as the tree of the knowledge of good and evil.

…

15 The Lord God took the man and placed him in the garden of Eden to work it and watch over it. 16 And the Lord God commanded the man, "You are free to eat from any tree of the garden, 17 but you must not eat from the tree of the knowledge of good and evil, for on the day you eat from it, you will certainly die." 18 Then the Lord God said, "It is not good for the man to be alone. I will make a helper corresponding to him." 19 The Lord God formed out of the ground every wild animal and every bird of the sky, and brought each to the man to see what he would call it. And whatever the man called a living creature, that was its name. 20 The man gave names to all the livestock, to the birds of the sky, and to every wild animal; but for the man no helper was found corresponding to him. 21 So the Lord God caused a deep sleep to come over the man, and he slept. God took one of his ribs and closed the flesh at that place. 22 Then the Lord God made the rib he had taken from the man into a woman and brought her to the man.

GENESIS 3:8-12, 22-24

SIN'S CONSEQUENCES

8 Then the man and his wife heard the sound of the Lord God walking in the garden at the time of

the evening breeze, and they hid from the LORD God among the trees of the garden. ⁹ So the LORD God called out to the man and said to him, "Where are you?"

¹⁰ And he said, "I heard you in the garden, and I was afraid because I was naked, so I hid."

¹¹ Then he asked, "Who told you that you were naked? Did you eat from the tree that I commanded you not to eat from?"

¹² The man replied, "The woman you gave to be with me—she gave me some fruit from the tree, and I ate."

…

²² The LORD God said, "Since the man has become like one of us, knowing good and evil, he must not reach out, take from the tree of life, eat, and live forever." ²³ So the LORD God sent him away from the garden of Eden to work the ground from which he was taken. ²⁴ He drove the man out and stationed the cherubim and the flaming, whirling sword east of the garden of Eden to guard the way to the tree of life.

GENESIS 4:1–16

CAIN MURDERS ABEL

¹ The man was intimate with his wife Eve, and she conceived and gave birth to Cain. She said, "I have had a male child with the LORD's help." ² She also gave birth to his brother Abel. Now Abel became a shepherd of flocks, but Cain worked the ground. ³ In the course of time Cain presented some of the land's produce as an offering to the LORD. ⁴ And Abel also presented an offering—some of the firstborn of his flock and their fat portions. The LORD had regard for Abel and his offering, ⁵ but he did not have regard for Cain and his offering. Cain was furious, and he looked despondent.

⁶ Then the LORD said to Cain, "Why are you furious? And why do you look despondent? ⁷ If you do what is right, won't you be accepted? But if you do not do what is right, sin is crouching at the door. Its desire is for you, but you must rule over it."

⁸ Cain said to his brother Abel, "Let's go out to the field." And while they were in the field, Cain attacked his brother Abel and killed him.

NOTES

NOTES

⁹ Then the LORD said to Cain, "Where is your brother Abel?"

"I don't know," he replied. "Am I my brother's guardian?"

¹⁰ Then he said, "What have you done? Your brother's blood cries out to me from the ground! ¹¹ So now you are cursed, alienated from the ground that opened its mouth to receive your brother's blood you have shed. ¹² If you work the ground, it will never again give you its yield. You will be a restless wanderer on the earth."

¹³ But Cain answered the LORD, "My punishment is too great to bear! ¹⁴ Since you are banishing me today from the face of the earth, and I must hide from your presence and become a restless wanderer on the earth, whoever finds me will kill me."

¹⁵ Then the LORD replied to him, "In that case, whoever kills Cain will suffer vengeance seven times over." And he placed a mark on Cain so that whoever found him would not kill him.

> ¹⁶ Then Cain went out from the LORD's presence and lived in the land of Nod, east of Eden.

ROMANS 5:12

Therefore, just as sin entered the world through one man, and death through sin, in this way death spread to all people, because all sinned.

NOTES

DATE

DAY 9

GOD LEADS HIS PEOPLE INTO HIS PRESENCE

God's presence was with Moses and with Israel as they were brought out of slavery in Egypt.

EXODUS 3:1-15

MOSES AND THE BURNING BUSH

¹ Meanwhile, Moses was shepherding the flock of his father-in-law Jethro, the priest of Midian. He led the flock to the far side of the wilderness and came to Horeb, the mountain of God. ² Then the angel of the Lord appeared to him in a flame of fire within a bush. As Moses looked, he saw that the bush was on fire but was not consumed. ³ So Moses thought, "I must go over and look at this remarkable sight. Why isn't the bush burning up?"

⁴ When the Lord saw that he had gone over to look, God called out to him from the bush, "Moses, Moses!"

"Here I am," he answered.

⁵ "Do not come closer," he said. "Remove the sandals from your feet, for the place where you are standing is holy ground." ⁶ Then he continued, "I am the God of your father, the God of Abraham, the God of Isaac, and the God of Jacob." Moses hid his face because he was afraid to look at God.

⁷ Then the Lord said, "I have observed the misery of my people in Egypt, and have heard them crying out because of their oppressors. I know about their sufferings, ⁸ and I have come down to rescue them from the power of the Egyptians and to bring them from that land to a good and spacious land, a land flowing with milk and honey—the territory of the Canaanites, Hethites, Amorites, Perizzites, Hivites, and Jebusites. ⁹ So because the Israelites' cry for help has come to me, and I have also seen the way the Egyptians are oppressing them, ¹⁰ therefore, go. I am sending you to Pharaoh so that you may lead my people, the Israelites, out of Egypt."

¹¹ But Moses asked God, "Who am I that I should go to Pharaoh and that I should bring the Israelites out of Egypt?"

¹² He answered, "I will certainly be with you, and this will be the sign to you that I am the one who sent you: when you bring the people out of Egypt, you will all worship God at this mountain."

¹³ Then Moses asked God, "If I go to the Israelites and say to them, 'The God of your ancestors has sent me to you,' and they ask me, 'What is his name?' what should I tell them?"

¹⁴ God replied to Moses, "I AM WHO I AM. This is what you are to say to the Israelites: I AM has sent me to you." ¹⁵ God also said to Moses, "Say this to the Israelites: The Lord, the God of your ancestors, the God of Abraham, the God of Isaac, and the God of Jacob, has sent me to you. This is my name forever; this is how I am to be remembered in every generation."

EXODUS 6:1-8

¹ But the Lord replied to Moses, "Now you will see what I will do to Pharaoh: because of a strong hand he will let them go, and because of a strong hand he will drive them from his land."

GOD PROMISES FREEDOM

² Then God spoke to Moses, telling him, "I am the Lord. ³ I appeared to Abraham, Isaac, and Jacob as God Almighty, but I was not known to them by my name 'the Lord.' ⁴ I also established my covenant with them to give them the land of Canaan, the land they lived in as aliens. ⁵ Furthermore, I have heard the groaning of the Israelites, whom the Egyptians are forcing to work as slaves, and I have remembered my covenant.

⁶ "Therefore tell the Israelites: I am the Lord, and I will bring you out from the forced labor of the Egyptians and rescue you from slavery to them. I will redeem you with an outstretched arm and great acts of judgment. ⁷ I will take you as my people, and I will be your God. You will know that I am the Lord your God, who brought you out from the forced labor of the Egyptians. ⁸ I will bring you to the land that I swore to give to Abraham, Isaac, and Jacob, and I will give it to you as a possession. I am the Lord."

NOTES

NOTES

EXODUS 13:17-22

THE ROUTE OF THE EXODUS

[17] When Pharaoh let the people go, God did not lead them along the road to the land of the Philistines, even though it was nearby; for God said, "The people will change their minds and return to Egypt if they face war." [18] So he led the people around toward the Red Sea along the road of the wilderness. And the Israelites left the land of Egypt in battle formation.

[19] Moses took the bones of Joseph with him, because Joseph had made the Israelites swear a solemn oath, saying, "God will certainly come to your aid; then you must take my bones with you from this place."

[20] They set out from Succoth and camped at Etham on the edge of the wilderness. [21] The LORD went ahead of them in a pillar of cloud to lead them on their way during the day and in a pillar of fire to give them light at night, so that they could travel day or night. [22] The pillar of cloud by day and the pillar of fire by night never left its place in front of the people.

EXODUS 15:1-3, 17

ISRAEL'S SONG

[1] Then Moses and the Israelites sang this song to the LORD. They said:

> I will sing to the LORD,
> for he is highly exalted;
> he has thrown the horse
> and its rider into the sea.
> [2] The LORD is my strength and my song;
> he has become my salvation.
> This is my God, and I will praise him,
> my father's God, and I will exalt him.
> [3] The LORD is a warrior;
> the LORD is his name.
>
> ...
>
> [17] You will bring them in and plant them
> on the mountain of your possession;
> LORD, you have prepared the place
> for your dwelling;
> Lord, your hands have established the sanctuary.

JEREMIAH 7:22-23

[22] "…for when I brought your ancestors out of the land of Egypt, I did not speak with them or command them concerning burnt offering and sacrifice. [23] However, I did give them this command: 'Obey me, and then I will be your God, and you will be my people. Follow every way I command you so that it may go well with you.'"

MOUNTAINS OF GOD

In the ancient Near East, people thought of mountains as the domain of the gods. Closer to the sky than other parts of creation, they believed mountaintops were places where heaven and earth met. Mountains were considered appropriate dwelling places for powerful, divine beings.

In Scripture, God often used mountains or elevated places to meet with His people. Here are several examples where mountains served this purpose, along with references for further study.

THE GARDEN OF EDEN

Though the book of Genesis does not tell us that Eden was atop a mountain, the prophet Ezekiel does. There, "Eden, the garden of God" is also called "the holy mountain of God."

Ezk 28:13-16

A MOUNTAIN IN MORIAH

God told Abraham to go to a mountain in the land of Moriah to sacrifice his son Isaac. It was there on that mountain, with a ram caught in a thicket, that God revealed Himself to be the one who provides.

Gn 22:1-19

MOUNT SINAI

Mount Sinai, also called Horeb, was frequently used as a meeting place between God and His people—first with Moses, then also with Aaron, Nadab, Abihu, the seventy elders of Israel, and years later, with Elijah.

Ex 3:1-4:17; 19:1-34:30; 24:1-18; 1Kg 19:8-18

MOUNT NEBO

In the book of Deuteronomy, God told Moses to ascend Mount Nebo. There, Moses was given a view of the promised land before he died.

Dt 32:49; 34:1

MOUNT CARMEL

Elijah had a mountaintop experience with the Lord when he challenged the prophets of Baal to a contest atop Mount Carmel. There, God revealed Himself to His people with fire from heaven.

1Kg 18:20–40

MOUNT ZION

Mount Zion is where Solomon built the temple to the Lord in Jerusalem. Therefore, Zion is called God's holy mountain.

Ps 48:1

NEW JERUSALEM

In the book of Revelation, John was carried in the Spirit to "a great, high mountain" to witness New Jerusalem coming down from heaven.

Rv 21:10

MOUNTAINS IN JESUS'S MINISTRY

Jesus preached a sermon on a mountain, much like the way Moses delivered the Law to the people from Mount Sinai.

Mt 5–7

Jesus often went up on a mountain to pray or to be alone.

Mt 14:23; Mk 6:46; Lk 6:12; 9:28; Jn 6:15

Jesus was on a mountain when He appointed the Twelve.

Mk 3:13; Lk 6:12–16

Jesus went up on a mountain before and after feeding the five thousand.

Jn 6:3–15

Jesus was on a mountain when He healed people and then fed four thousand.

Mt 15:29–39

Jesus was transfigured on a mountain where He met with Moses and Elijah.

Mt 17:1–8; Mk 9:2–8; Lk 9:28–36

Jesus and His disciples were on the Mount of Olives when He told them about the end of the age.

Mt 24–25

From on top of a mountain in Galilee, Jesus commissioned the Eleven to make disciples of all nations.

Mt 28:16–20

DAY 10

GOD'S PRESENCE TRANSFORMS HIS PEOPLE

Like Moses's face made radiant by standing in God's presence on Mt. Sinai, God's people are transformed by life in His presence.

EXODUS 19:1-9, 16-20

ISRAEL AT SINAI

¹ In the third month from the very day the Israelites left the land of Egypt, they came to the Sinai Wilderness. ² They traveled from Rephidim, came to the Sinai Wilderness, and camped in the wilderness. Israel camped there in front of the mountain.

³ Moses went up the mountain to God, and the LORD called to him from the mountain: "This is what you must say to the house of Jacob and explain to the Israelites: ⁴ 'You have seen what I did to the Egyptians and how I carried you on eagles' wings and brought you to myself. ⁵ Now if you will carefully listen to me and keep my covenant, you will be my own possession out of all the peoples, although the whole earth is mine, ⁶ and you will be my kingdom of priests and my holy nation.' These are the words that you are to say to the Israelites."

⁷ After Moses came back, he summoned the elders of the people and set before them all these words that the LORD had commanded him. ⁸ Then all the people responded together, "We will do all that the LORD has spoken." So Moses brought the people's words back to the LORD.

⁹ The LORD said to Moses, "I am going to come to you in a dense cloud, so that the people will hear when I speak with you and will always believe you." Moses reported the people's words to the LORD…

…

¹⁶ On the third day, when morning came, there was thunder and lightning, a thick cloud on the mountain, and a very loud blast from a ram's horn, so that all the people in the camp shuddered. ¹⁷ Then Moses brought the people out of the camp to meet God, and they stood at the foot of the mountain. ¹⁸ Mount Sinai was completely enveloped in smoke because the LORD came down on it in fire. Its smoke went up like the smoke of a furnace, and the whole mountain shook violently. ¹⁹ As the sound of the ram's horn grew louder and louder, Moses spoke and God answered him in the thunder.

²⁰ The LORD came down on Mount Sinai at the top of the mountain. Then the LORD summoned Moses to the top of the mountain, and he went up.

NOTES

NOTES

EXODUS 34:5-14, 27-35

⁵ The Lord came down in a cloud, stood with him there, and proclaimed his name, "the Lord." ⁶ The Lord passed in front of him and proclaimed:

> The Lord—the Lord is a compassionate and gracious God, slow to anger and abounding in faithful love and truth, ⁷ maintaining faithful love to a thousand generations, forgiving iniquity, rebellion, and sin. But he will not leave the guilty unpunished, bringing the consequences of the fathers' iniquity on the children and grandchildren to the third and fourth generation.

⁸ Moses immediately knelt low on the ground and worshiped. ⁹ Then he said, "My Lord, if I have indeed found favor with you, my Lord, please go with us (even though this is a stiff-necked people), forgive our iniquity and our sin, and accept us as your own possession."

COVENANT OBLIGATIONS

¹⁰ And the Lord responded, "Look, I am making a covenant. In the presence of all your people I will perform wonders that have never been done in the whole earth or in any nation. All the people you live among will see the Lord's work, for what I am doing with you is awe-inspiring. ¹¹ Observe what I command you today. I am going to drive out before you the Amorites, Canaanites, Hethites, Perizzites, Hivites, and Jebusites. ¹² Be careful not to make a treaty with the inhabitants of the land that you are going to enter; otherwise, they will become a snare among you. ¹³ Instead, you must tear down their altars, smash their sacred pillars, and chop down their Asherah poles. ¹⁴ Because the Lord is jealous for his reputation, you are never to bow down to another god. He is a jealous God.

...

²⁷ The Lord also said to Moses, "Write down these words, for I have made a covenant with you and with Israel based on these words."

²⁸ Moses was there with the Lord forty days and forty nights; he did not eat food or drink water. He wrote the Ten Commandments, the words of the covenant, on the tablets.

MOSES'S RADIANT FACE

²⁹ As Moses descended from Mount Sinai—with the two tablets of the testimony in his hands as he descended the mountain—he did not realize

that the skin of his face shone as a result of his speaking with the LORD. ³⁰ When Aaron and all the Israelites saw Moses, the skin of his face shone! They were afraid to come near him. ³¹ But Moses called out to them, so Aaron and all the leaders of the community returned to him, and Moses spoke to them. ³² Afterward all the Israelites came near, and he commanded them to do everything the LORD had told him on Mount Sinai. ³³ When Moses had finished speaking with them, he put a veil over his face. ³⁴ But whenever Moses went before the LORD to speak with him, he would remove the veil until he came out. After he came out, he would tell the Israelites what he had been commanded, ³⁵ and the Israelites would see that Moses's face was radiant. Then Moses would put the veil over his face again until he went to speak with the LORD.

2 CORINTHIANS 3:7–18

NEW COVENANT MINISTRY

⁷ Now if the ministry that brought death, chiseled in letters on stones, came with glory, so that the Israelites were not able to gaze steadily at Moses's face because of its glory, which was set aside, ⁸ how will the ministry of the Spirit not be more glorious? ⁹ For if the ministry that brought condemnation had glory, the ministry that brings righteousness overflows with even more glory. ¹⁰ In fact, what had been glorious is not glorious now by comparison because of the glory that surpasses it. ¹¹ For if what was set aside was glorious, what endures will be even more glorious.

¹² Since, then, we have such a hope, we act with great boldness. ¹³ We are not like Moses, who used to put a veil over his face to prevent the Israelites from gazing steadily until the end of the glory of what was being set aside, ¹⁴ but their minds were hardened. For to this day, at the reading of the old covenant, the same veil remains; it is not lifted, because it is set aside only in Christ. ¹⁵ Yet still today, whenever Moses is read, a veil lies over their hearts, ¹⁶ but whenever a person turns to the Lord, the veil is removed. ¹⁷ Now the Lord is the Spirit, and where the Spirit of the Lord is, there is freedom. ¹⁸ We all, with unveiled faces, are looking as in a mirror at the glory of the Lord and are being transformed into the same image from glory to glory; this is from the Lord who is the Spirit.

NOTES

DAY 11

GOD DWELLS AMONG HIS PEOPLE IN THE TABERNACLE

God provided a place for His people to draw near to Him.

EXODUS 25:1–22

OFFERINGS TO BUILD THE TABERNACLE

¹ The LORD spoke to Moses: ² "Tell the Israelites to take an offering for me. You are to take my offering from everyone who is willing to give. ³ This is the offering you are to receive from them: gold, silver, and bronze; ⁴ blue, purple, and scarlet yarn; fine linen and goat hair; ⁵ ram skins dyed red and fine leather; acacia wood; ⁶ oil for the light; spices for the anointing oil and for the fragrant incense; ⁷ and onyx along with other gemstones for mounting on the ephod and breastpiece.

⁸ "They are to make a sanctuary for me so that I may dwell among them. ⁹ You must make it according to all that I show you—the pattern of the tabernacle as well as the pattern of all its furnishings.

THE ARK

¹⁰ "They are to make an ark of acacia wood, forty-five inches long, twenty-seven inches wide, and twenty-seven inches high. ¹¹ Overlay it with pure gold; overlay it both inside and out. Also make a gold molding all around it. ¹² Cast four gold rings for it and place them on its four feet, two rings on one side and two rings on the other side. ¹³ Make poles of acacia wood and overlay them with gold. ¹⁴ Insert the poles into the rings on the sides of the ark in order to carry the ark with them. ¹⁵ The poles are to remain in the rings of the ark; they must not be removed from it. ¹⁶ Put the tablets of the testimony that I will give you into the ark. ¹⁷ Make a mercy seat of pure gold, forty-five inches long and twenty-seven inches wide. ¹⁸ Make two cherubim of gold; make them of hammered work at the two ends of the mercy seat. ¹⁹ Make one cherub at one end and one cherub at the other end. At its two ends, make the cherubim of one piece with the mercy seat. ²⁰ The cherubim are to have wings spread out above, covering the mercy seat with their wings, and are to face one another. The faces of the cherubim should be toward the mercy seat. ²¹ Set the mercy seat on top of the ark and put the tablets of the testimony that I will give you into the ark. ²² I will meet with you there above the mercy seat, between the two cherubim that are over the ark of the testimony; I will speak with you from there about all that I command you regarding the Israelites."

EXODUS 26:31–35

³¹ "You are to make a curtain of blue, purple, and scarlet yarn, and finely spun linen with a design of cherubim worked into it. ³² Hang it on four

NOTES

gold-plated pillars of acacia wood that have gold hooks and that stand on four silver bases. ³³ Hang the curtain under the clasps and bring the ark of the testimony there behind the curtain, so the curtain will make a separation for you between the holy place and the most holy place. ³⁴ Put the mercy seat on the ark of the testimony in the most holy place. ³⁵ Place the table outside the curtain and the lampstand on the south side of the tabernacle, opposite the table; put the table on the north side."

EXODUS 40:31-38

³¹ Moses, Aaron, and his sons washed their hands and feet from it. ³² They washed whenever they came to the tent of meeting and approached the altar, just as the LORD had commanded Moses.

³³ Next Moses set up the surrounding courtyard for the tabernacle and the altar and hung a screen for the gate of the courtyard. So Moses finished the work.

THE LORD'S GLORY

³⁴ **The cloud covered the tent of meeting, and the glory of the LORD filled the tabernacle.**

³⁵ Moses was unable to enter the tent of meeting because the cloud rested on it, and the glory of the LORD filled the tabernacle.

³⁶ The Israelites set out whenever the cloud was taken up from the tabernacle throughout all the stages of their journey. ³⁷ If the cloud was not taken up, they did not set out until the day it was taken up. ³⁸ For the cloud of the LORD was over the tabernacle by day, and there was a fire inside the cloud by night, visible to the entire house of Israel throughout all the stages of their journey.

NUMBERS 10:33-36

³³ They set out from the mountain of the LORD on a three-day journey with the ark of the LORD's covenant traveling ahead of them for those three days to seek a resting place for them. ³⁴ Meanwhile, the cloud of the LORD was over them by day when they set out from the camp.

³⁵ Whenever the ark set out, Moses would say:

> Arise, Lord!
> Let your enemies be scattered,
> and those who hate you flee from your presence.

³⁶ When it came to rest, he would say:

> Return, Lord,
> to the countless thousands of Israel.

HEBREWS 8:1–5

¹ Now the main point of what is being said is this: We have this kind of high priest, who sat down at the right hand of the throne of the Majesty in the heavens, ² a minister of the sanctuary and the true tabernacle that was set up by the Lord and not man. ³ For every high priest is appointed to offer gifts and sacrifices; therefore, it was necessary for this priest also to have something to offer. ⁴ Now if he were on earth, he wouldn't be a priest, since there are those offering the gifts prescribed by the law. ⁵ These serve as a copy and shadow of the heavenly things, as Moses was warned when he was about to complete the tabernacle. For God said, Be careful that you make everything according to the pattern that was shown to you on the mountain.

DAY 12

GOD'S PRESENCE FILLS THE TEMPLE

God's presence filled the temple, and His people drew near and worshiped Him.

1 KINGS 8:1–13, 22–53

SOLOMON'S DEDICATION OF THE TEMPLE

¹ At that time Solomon assembled the elders of Israel, all the tribal heads and the ancestral leaders of the Israelites before him at Jerusalem in order to bring the ark of the Lord's covenant from the city of David, that is Zion. ² So all the men of Israel were assembled in the presence of King Solomon in the month of Ethanim, which is the seventh month, at the festival.

³ All the elders of Israel came, and the priests picked up the ark. ⁴ The priests and the Levites brought the ark of the Lord, the tent of meeting, and the holy utensils that were in the tent. ⁵ King Solomon and the entire congregation of Israel, who had gathered around him and were with him in front of the ark, were sacrificing sheep, goats, and cattle that could not be counted or numbered, because there were so many. ⁶ The priests brought the ark of the Lord's covenant to its place, into the inner sanctuary of the temple, to the most holy place beneath the wings of the cherubim. ⁷ For the cherubim were spreading their wings over the place of the ark, so that the cherubim covered the ark and its poles from above. ⁸ The poles were so long that their ends were seen from the holy place in front of the inner sanctuary, but they were not seen from outside the sanctuary; they are still there today. ⁹ Nothing was in the ark except the two stone tablets that Moses had put there at Horeb, where the Lord made a covenant with the Israelites when they came out of the land of Egypt.

¹⁰ When the priests came out of the holy place, the cloud filled the Lord's temple, ¹¹ and because of the cloud, the priests were not able to continue ministering, for the glory of the Lord filled the temple.

¹² Then Solomon said:

> The Lord said that he would dwell in total darkness.
> ¹³ I have indeed built an exalted temple for you,
> a place for your dwelling forever.

...

SOLOMON'S PRAYER

²² Then Solomon stood before the altar of the Lord in front of the entire congregation of Israel and spread out his hands toward heaven. ²³ He said:

> Lord God of Israel,
> there is no God like you
> in heaven above or on earth below,
> who keeps the gracious covenant
> with your servants who walk before you
> with all their heart.
> ²⁴ You have kept what you promised
> to your servant, my father David.
> You spoke directly to him
> and you fulfilled your promise by your power
> as it is today.
> ²⁵ Therefore, Lord God of Israel,
> keep what you promised
> to your servant, my father David:
> You will never fail to have a man
> to sit before me on the throne of Israel,
> if only your sons take care to walk before me
> as you have walked before me.
> ²⁶ Now Lord God of Israel,
> please confirm what you promised
> to your servant, my father David.

> ²⁷ But will God indeed live on earth?
> Even heaven, the highest heaven,
>   cannot contain you,
> much less this temple I have built.

NOTES

[28] Listen to your servant's prayer and his petition,
Lord my God,
so that you may hear the cry and the prayer
that your servant prays before you today,
[29] so that your eyes may watch over this temple night and day,
toward the place where you said,
"My name will be there,"
and so that you may hear the prayer
that your servant prays toward this place.
[30] Hear the petition of your servant
and your people Israel,
which they pray toward this place.
May you hear in your dwelling place in heaven.
May you hear and forgive.
[31] When a man sins against his neighbor
and is forced to take an oath,
and he comes to take an oath
before your altar in this temple,
[32] may you hear in heaven and act.
May you judge your servants,
condemning the wicked man by bringing
what he has done on his own head
and providing justice for the righteous
by rewarding him according to his righteousness.
[33] When your people Israel are defeated before an enemy,
because they have sinned against you,
and they return to you and praise your name,
and they pray and plead with you
for mercy in this temple,
[34] may you hear in heaven
and forgive the sin of your people Israel.
May you restore them to the land
you gave their ancestors.
[35] When the skies are shut and there is no rain,
because they have sinned against you,
and they pray toward this place
and praise your name,
and they turn from their sins
because you are afflicting them,
[36] may you hear in heaven
and forgive the sin of your servants

and your people Israel,
so that you may teach them to walk on the good way.
May you send rain on your land
that you gave your people for an inheritance.
⁳⁷ When there is famine in the land,
when there is pestilence,
when there is blight or mildew, locust or grasshopper,
when their enemy besieges them
in the land and its cities,
when there is any plague or illness,
³⁸ every prayer or petition
that any person or that all your people Israel may have—
they each know their own affliction—
as they spread out their hands toward this temple,
³⁹ may you hear in heaven, your dwelling place,
and may you forgive, act, and give to everyone
according to all their ways, since you know each heart,
for you alone know every human heart,
⁴⁰ so that they may fear you
all the days they live on the land
you gave our ancestors.
⁴¹ Even for the foreigner who is not of your people Israel
but has come from a distant land
because of your name—
⁴² for they will hear of your great name,
strong hand, and outstretched arm,
and will come and pray toward this temple—
⁴³ may you hear in heaven, your dwelling place,
and do according to all the foreigner asks.
Then all peoples of earth will know your name,
to fear you as your people Israel do
and to know that this temple I have built
bears your name.
⁴⁴ When your people go out to fight against their enemies,
wherever you send them,
and they pray to the Lord
in the direction of the city you have chosen
and the temple I have built for your name,
⁴⁵ may you hear their prayer and petition in heaven
and uphold their cause.
⁴⁶ When they sin against you—
for there is no one who does not sin—

NOTES

NOTES

and you are angry with them
and hand them over to the enemy,
and their captors deport them to the enemy's country—
whether distant or nearby—
⁴⁷ and when they come to their senses
in the land where they were deported
and repent and petition you in their captors' land:
"We have sinned and done wrong;
we have been wicked,"
⁴⁸ and when they return to you with all their heart and all their soul
in the land of their enemies who took them captive,
and when they pray to you in the direction of their land
that you gave their ancestors,
the city you have chosen,
and the temple I have built for your name,
⁴⁹ may you hear in heaven, your dwelling place,
their prayer and petition and uphold their cause.
⁵⁰ May you forgive your people
who sinned against you
and all their rebellions against you,
and may you grant them compassion
before their captors,
so that they may treat them compassionately.
⁵¹ For they are your people and your inheritance;
you brought them out of Egypt,
out of the middle of an iron furnace.
⁵² May your eyes be open to your servant's petition
and to the petition of your people Israel,
listening to them whenever they call to you.
⁵³ For you, Lord God, have set them apart as your inheritance
from all peoples of the earth,
as you spoke through your servant Moses
when you brought our ancestors out of Egypt.

2 CHRONICLES 7:1-3

THE DEDICATION CEREMONIES

¹ When Solomon finished praying, fire descended from heaven and consumed the burnt offering and the sacrifices, and the glory of the Lord filled the temple. ² The priests were not able to enter the Lord's temple

because the glory of the Lord filled the temple of the Lord. ³ All the Israelites were watching when the fire descended and the glory of the Lord came on the temple. They bowed down on the pavement with their faces to the ground. They worshiped and praised the Lord:

> For he is good,
> for his faithful love endures forever.

REVELATION 11:19

Then the temple of God in heaven was opened, and the ark of his covenant appeared in his temple. There were flashes of lightning, rumblings and peals of thunder, an earthquake, and severe hail.

GRACE DAY

Take this day to catch up on your reading,
pray, and rest in the presence of the Lord.

All the Israelites were watching when the fire descended and the glory of the LORD came on the temple. They bowed down on the pavement with their faces to the ground. They worshiped and praised the LORD:

For he is good,
for his faithful love endures forever.

2 CHRONICLES 7:3

DAY 13

DAY 14

WEEKLY

Scripture is God-breathed and true. When we memorize it, we carry the good news of Jesus with us wherever we go.

This week, we we will work on memorizing the second line of Psalm 73:28. Make a practice of repeating it to yourself as you go about your week, saying it out loud or thinking about it throughout the day.

TRUTH

WEEK 2

BUT AS FOR ME, GOD'S PRESENCE IS MY GOOD.

I HAVE MADE THE LORD GOD MY REFUGE,

SO I CAN TELL ABOUT ALL YOU DO.

Psalm 73:28

DAY 15

GOD'S PRESENCE LEAVES THE TEMPLE

When God's people turned away from Him, He removed His presence from the temple.

JEREMIAH 7:1–15, 21–31

FALSE TRUST IN THE TEMPLE

¹ This is the word that came to Jeremiah from the Lord: ² "Stand in the gate of the house of the Lord and there call out this word: 'Hear the word of the Lord, all you people of Judah who enter through these gates to worship the Lord.

³ "'This is what the Lord of Armies, the God of Israel, says: Correct your ways and your actions, and I will allow you to live in this place. ⁴ Do not trust deceitful words, chanting, "This is the temple of the Lord, the temple of the Lord, the temple of the Lord." ⁵ Instead, if you really correct your ways and your actions, if you act justly toward one another, ⁶ if you no longer oppress the resident alien, the fatherless, and the widow and no longer shed innocent blood in this place or follow other gods, bringing harm on yourselves, ⁷ I will allow you to live in this place, the land I gave to your ancestors long ago and forever. ⁸ But look, you keep trusting in deceitful words that cannot help.

⁹ "'Do you steal, murder, commit adultery, swear falsely, burn incense to Baal, and follow other gods that you have not known? ¹⁰ Then do you come and stand before me in this house that bears my name and say, "We are rescued, so we can continue doing all these detestable acts"? ¹¹ Has this house, which bears my name, become a den of robbers in your view? Yes, I too have seen it.

This is the Lord's declaration."

SHILOH AS A WARNING

¹² "'But return to my place that was at Shiloh, where I made my name dwell at first. See what I did to it because of the evil of my people Israel. ¹³ Now, because you have done all these things—

this is the Lord's declaration—and because I have spoken to you time and time again but you wouldn't listen, and I have called to you, but you wouldn't answer, ¹⁴ what I did to Shiloh I will do to the house that bears my name, the house in which you trust, the place that I gave you and your ancestors. ¹⁵ I will banish you from my presence, just as I banished all of your brothers, all the descendants of Ephraim.'"

…

OBEDIENCE OVER SACRIFICE

²¹ This is what the Lord of Armies, the God of Israel, says: "Add your burnt offerings to your other sacrifices, and eat the meat yourselves, ²² for when I brought your ancestors out of the land of Egypt, I did not speak with them or command them concerning burnt offering and sacrifice. ²³ However, I did give them this command: 'Obey me, and then I will be your God, and you will be my people. Follow every way I command you so that it may go well with you.' ²⁴ Yet they didn't listen or pay attention but followed their own advice and their own stubborn, evil heart. They went backward and not forward. ²⁵ Since the day your ancestors came out of the land of Egypt until today, I have sent all my servants the prophets to you time and time again. ²⁶ However, my people wouldn't listen to me or pay attention but became obstinate; they did more evil than their ancestors.

A LAMENT FOR DISOBEDIENT JUDAH

²⁷ "When you speak all these things to them, they will not listen to you. When you call to them, they will not answer you. ²⁸ Therefore, declare to them, 'This is the nation that would not listen to the Lord their God and would not accept discipline. Truth has perished—it has disappeared from their mouths. ²⁹ Cut off the hair of your sacred vow and throw it away. Raise up a dirge on the barren heights, for the Lord has rejected and abandoned the generation under his wrath.'

³⁰ "For the Judeans have done what is evil in my sight." This is the Lord's declaration. "They have set up their abhorrent things in the house that bears my name in order to defile it. ³¹ They have built the high places of Topheth in Ben Hinnom Valley in order to burn their sons and daughters in the fire, a thing I did not command; I never entertained the thought."

NOTES

NOTES

2 CHRONICLES 7:19–21

[19] "However, if you turn away and abandon my statutes and my commands that I have set before you and if you go and serve other gods and bow in worship to them, [20] then I will uproot Israel from the soil that I gave them, and this temple that I have sanctified for my name I will banish from my presence; I will make it an object of scorn and ridicule among all the peoples. [21] As for this temple, which was exalted, everyone who passes by will be appalled and will say, Why did the Lord do this to this land and this temple?"

EZEKIEL 10

GOD'S GLORY LEAVES THE TEMPLE

[1] Then I looked, and there above the expanse over the heads of the cherubim was something like a throne with the appearance of lapis lazuli. [2] The Lord spoke to the man clothed in linen and said, "Go inside the wheelwork beneath the cherubim. Fill your hands with blazing coals from among the cherubim and scatter them over the city." So he went in as I watched.

[3] Now the cherubim were standing to the south of the temple when the man went in, and the cloud filled the inner court. [4] Then the glory of the Lord rose from above the cherub to the threshold of the temple. The temple was filled with the cloud, and the court was filled with the brightness of the Lord's glory. [5] The sound of the cherubim's wings could be heard as far as the outer court; it was like the voice of God Almighty when he speaks.

[6] After the Lord commanded the man clothed in linen, saying, "Take fire from inside the wheelwork, from among the cherubim," the man went in and stood beside a wheel. [7] Then the cherub reached out his hand to the fire that was among them. He took some and put it into the hands of the man clothed in linen, who took it and went out. [8] The cherubim appeared to have the form of human hands under their wings.

[9] I looked, and there were four wheels beside the cherubim, one wheel beside each cherub. The luster of the wheels was like the gleam of beryl. [10] In appearance, all four looked alike, like a wheel within a wheel. [11] When they moved, they would go in any of the four directions, without pivoting as they moved. But wherever the head faced, they would go

in that direction, without pivoting as they went. ¹² Their entire bodies, including their backs, hands, wings, and the wheels that the four of them had, were full of eyes all around. ¹³ As I listened the wheels were called "the wheelwork." ¹⁴ Each one had four faces: one was the face of a cherub, the second the face of a human, the third the face of a lion, and the fourth the face of an eagle.

¹⁵ The cherubim ascended; these were the living creatures I had seen by the Chebar Canal. ¹⁶ When the cherubim moved, the wheels moved beside them, and when they lifted their wings to rise from the earth, even then the wheels did not veer away from them. ¹⁷ When the cherubim stopped, the wheels stood still, and when they ascended, the wheels ascended with them, for the spirit of the living creatures was in them.

¹⁸ Then the glory of the Lord moved away from the threshold of the temple and stopped above the cherubim. ¹⁹ The cherubim lifted their wings and ascended from the earth right before my eyes; the wheels were beside them as they went. The glory of the God of Israel was above them, and it stopped at the entrance to the eastern gate of the Lord's house.

²⁰ These were the living creatures I had seen beneath the God of Israel by the Chebar Canal, and I recognized that they were cherubim. ²¹ Each had four faces and each had four wings, with what looked something like human hands under their wings. ²² Their faces looked like the same faces I had seen by the Chebar Canal. Each creature went straight ahead.

HAGGAI 2:6–9

⁶ For the Lord of Armies says this: "Once more, in a little while, I am going to shake the heavens and the earth, the sea and the dry land. ⁷ I will shake all the nations so that the treasures of all the nations will come, and I will fill this house with glory," says the Lord of Armies. ⁸ "The silver and gold belong to me"—this is the declaration of the Lord of Armies. ⁹ "The final glory of this house will be greater than the first," says the Lord of Armies.

> "I will provide peace in this place"—this is the declaration of the Lord of Armies.

NOTES

DAY 16

ONE GREATER THAN THE TEMPLE

The presence of
God came to earth and
dwelt among people in
Jesus Christ.

JOHN 1:1-3, 14

¹ In the beginning was the Word, and the Word was with God, and the Word was God. ² He was with God in the beginning. ³ All things were created through him, and apart from him not one thing was created that has been created.

…

¹⁴ The Word became flesh and dwelt among us. We observed his glory, the glory as the one and only Son from the Father, full of grace and truth.

LUKE 2:25-32

SIMEON'S PROPHETIC PRAISE

²⁵ There was a man in Jerusalem whose name was Simeon. This man was righteous and devout, looking forward to Israel's consolation, and the Holy Spirit was on him. ²⁶ It had been revealed to him by the Holy Spirit that he would not see death before he saw the Lord's Messiah. ²⁷ Guided by the Spirit, he entered the temple. When the parents brought in the child Jesus to perform for him what was customary under the law, ²⁸ Simeon took him up in his arms, praised God, and said,

> ²⁹ Now, Master,
> you can dismiss your servant in peace,
> as you promised.
> ³⁰ For my eyes have seen your salvation.
> ³¹ You have prepared it
> in the presence of all peoples—
> ³² a light for revelation to the Gentiles
> and glory to your people Israel.

MATTHEW 12:3-8

³ He said to them, "Haven't you read what David did when he and those who were with him were hungry: ⁴ how he entered the house of God, and they ate the bread of the Presence—which is not lawful for him or for those with him to eat, but only for the priests? ⁵ Or haven't you read in the law that on Sabbath days the priests in the temple violate the Sabbath and are innocent? ⁶ I tell you that something greater than the temple is here. ⁷ If you had known what this means, I desire mercy and not sacrifice, you would not have condemned the innocent. ⁸ For the Son of Man is Lord of the Sabbath."

NOTES

NOTES

JOHN 2:14-22

[14] In the temple he found people selling oxen, sheep, and doves, and he also found the money changers sitting there. [15] After making a whip out of cords, he drove everyone out of the temple with their sheep and oxen. He also poured out the money changers' coins and overturned the tables. [16] He told those who were selling doves, "Get these things out of here! Stop turning my Father's house into a marketplace!"

[17] And his disciples remembered that it is written: Zeal for your house will consume me.

[18] So the Jews replied to him, "What sign will you show us for doing these things?"

[19] Jesus answered, "Destroy this temple, and I will raise it up in three days."

[20] Therefore the Jews said, "This temple took forty-six years to build, and will you raise it up in three days?"

[21] But he was speaking about the temple of his body. [22] So when he was raised from the dead, his disciples remembered that he had said this, and they believed the Scripture and the statement Jesus had made.

MATTHEW 26:57-66

JESUS FACES THE SANHEDRIN

[57] Those who had arrested Jesus led him away to Caiaphas the high priest, where the scribes and the elders had convened. [58] Peter was following him at a distance right to the high priest's courtyard. He went in and was sitting with the servants to see the outcome.

[59] The chief priests and the whole Sanhedrin were looking for false testimony against Jesus so that they could put him to death, [60] but they could not find any, even though many false witnesses came forward. Finally, two who came forward [61] stated, "This man said, 'I can destroy the temple of God and rebuild it in three days.'"

[62] The high priest stood up and said to him, "Don't you have an answer to what these men are testifying against you?" [63] But Jesus kept silent. The

high priest said to him, "I charge you under oath by the living God: Tell us if you are the Messiah, the Son of God."

⁶⁴ "You have said it," Jesus told him. "But I tell you, in the future you will see the Son of Man seated at the right hand of Power and coming on the clouds of heaven."

⁶⁵ Then the high priest tore his robes and said, "He has blasphemed! Why do we still need witnesses? See, now you've heard the blasphemy. ⁶⁶ What is your decision?"

They answered, "He deserves death!"

MATTHEW 27:39-40

³⁹ Those who passed by were yelling insults at him, shaking their heads ⁴⁰ and saying, "You who would destroy the temple and rebuild it in three days, save yourself! If you are the Son of God, come down from the cross!"

MARK 15:33-39

THE DEATH OF JESUS

³³ When it was noon, darkness came over the whole land until three in the afternoon. ³⁴ And at three Jesus cried out with a loud voice, *"Eloi, Eloi, lemá sabachtháni?"* which is translated, "My God, my God, why have you abandoned me?"

³⁵ When some of those standing there heard this, they said, "See, he's calling for Elijah."

³⁶ Someone ran and filled a sponge with sour wine, fixed it on a stick, offered him a drink, and said, "Let's see if Elijah comes to take him down."

³⁷ Jesus let out a loud cry and breathed his last. ³⁸ Then the curtain of the temple was torn in two from top to bottom. ³⁹ When the centurion, who was standing opposite him, saw the way he breathed his last, he said, "Truly this man was the Son of God!"

NOTES

DAY 17

THE POURING OUT OF GOD'S SPIRIT

On the day of Pentecost, God's presence was poured out on believers.

ISAIAH 32:14–18

NOTES

¹⁴ For the palace will be deserted,
the busy city abandoned.
The hill and the watchtower will become
barren places forever,
the joy of wild donkeys,
and a pasture for flocks,
¹⁵ until the Spirit from on high is poured out on us.
Then the desert will become an orchard,
and the orchard will seem like a forest.
¹⁶ Then justice will inhabit the wilderness,
and righteousness will dwell in the orchard.

¹⁷ The result of righteousness will be peace;
the effect of righteousness
will be quiet confidence forever.
¹⁸ Then my people will dwell in a peaceful place,
in safe and secure dwellings.

ISAIAH 44:3–4

³ "For I will pour water on the thirsty land
and streams on the dry ground;
I will pour out my Spirit on your descendants
and my blessing on your offspring.
⁴ They will sprout among the grass
like poplars by flowing streams."

EZEKIEL 39:29

"I will no longer hide my face from them, for I will pour out my Spirit on the house of Israel." This is the declaration of the Lord God.

JOEL 2:28–32

GOD'S PROMISE OF HIS SPIRIT

²⁸ "After this
I will pour out my Spirit on all humanity;
then your sons and your daughters will prophesy,
your old men will have dreams,
and your young men will see visions.

NOTES

²⁹ I will even pour out my Spirit
on the male and female slaves in those days.
³⁰ I will display wonders
in the heavens and on the earth:
blood, fire, and columns of smoke.
³¹ The sun will be turned to darkness
and the moon to blood
before the great and terrible day of the Lord comes.
³² Then everyone who calls
on the name of the Lord will be saved,
for there will be an escape
for those on Mount Zion and in Jerusalem,
as the Lord promised,
among the survivors the Lord calls."

ACTS 2

PENTECOST

¹ When the day of Pentecost had arrived, they were all together in one place. ² Suddenly a sound like that of a violent rushing wind came from heaven, and it filled the whole house where they were staying. ³ They saw tongues like flames of fire that separated and rested on each one of them.

⁴ Then they were all filled with the Holy Spirit and began to speak in different tongues, as the Spirit enabled them.

⁵ Now there were Jews staying in Jerusalem, devout people from every nation under heaven. ⁶ When this sound occurred, a crowd came together and was confused because each one heard them speaking in his own language. ⁷ They were astounded and amazed, saying, "Look, aren't all these who are speaking Galileans? ⁸ How is it that each of us can hear them in our own native language? ⁹ Parthians, Medes, Elamites; those who live in Mesopotamia, in Judea and Cappadocia, Pontus and Asia, ¹⁰ Phrygia and Pamphylia, Egypt and the parts of Libya near Cyrene; visitors from Rome (both Jews and converts), ¹¹ Cretans and Arabs—we hear them declaring the magnificent acts of God in our own tongues." ¹² They were all astounded and perplexed, saying to one another, "What does this mean?" ¹³ But some sneered and said, "They're drunk on new wine."

PETER'S SERMON

¹⁴ Peter stood up with the Eleven, raised his voice, and proclaimed to them, "Fellow Jews and all you residents of Jerusalem, let this be known to you and pay attention to my words. ¹⁵ For these people are not drunk, as you suppose, since it's only nine in the morning. ¹⁶ On the contrary, this is what was spoken through the prophet Joel:

> ¹⁷ And it will be in the last days, says God,
> that I will pour out my Spirit on all people;
> then your sons and your daughters will prophesy,
> your young men will see visions,
> and your old men will dream dreams.
> ¹⁸ I will even pour out my Spirit
> on my servants in those days, both men and women
> and they will prophesy.
> ¹⁹ I will display wonders in the heaven above
> and signs on the earth below:
> blood and fire and a cloud of smoke.
> ²⁰ The sun will be turned to darkness
> and the moon to blood
> before the great and glorious day of the Lord comes.
> ²¹ Then everyone who calls
> on the name of the Lord will be saved.

²² "Fellow Israelites, listen to these words: This Jesus of Nazareth was a man attested to you by God with miracles, wonders, and signs that God did among you through him, just as you yourselves know. ²³ Though he was delivered up according to God's determined plan and foreknowledge, you used lawless people to nail him to a cross and kill him. ²⁴ God raised him up, ending the pains of death, because it was not possible for him to be held by death. ²⁵ For David says of him:

> I saw the Lord ever before me;
> because he is at my right hand,
> I will not be shaken.
> ²⁶ Therefore my heart is glad
> and my tongue rejoices.
> Moreover, my flesh will rest in hope,
> ²⁷ because you will not abandon me in Hades
> or allow your holy one to see decay.

NOTES

²⁸ You have revealed the paths of life to me;
you will fill me with gladness
in your presence.

²⁹ "Brothers and sisters, I can confidently speak to you about the patriarch David: He is both dead and buried, and his tomb is with us to this day. ³⁰ Since he was a prophet, he knew that God had sworn an oath to him to seat one of his descendants on his throne. ³¹ Seeing what was to come, he spoke concerning the resurrection of the Messiah: He was not abandoned in Hades, and his flesh did not experience decay.

³² "God has raised this Jesus; we are all witnesses of this. ³³ Therefore, since he has been exalted to the right hand of God and has received from the Father the promised Holy Spirit, he has poured out what you both see and hear. ³⁴ For it was not David who ascended into the heavens, but he himself says:

The Lord declared to my Lord,
'Sit at my right hand
³⁵ until I make your enemies your footstool.'

³⁶ "Therefore let all the house of Israel know with certainty that God has made this Jesus, whom you crucified, both Lord and Messiah."

CALL TO REPENTANCE

³⁷ When they heard this, they were pierced to the heart and said to Peter and the rest of the apostles, "Brothers, what should we do?"

³⁸ Peter replied, "Repent and be baptized, each of you, in the name of Jesus Christ for the forgiveness of your sins, and you will receive the gift of the Holy Spirit. ³⁹ For the promise is for you and for your children, and for all who are far off, as many as the Lord our God will call." ⁴⁰ With many other words he testified and strongly urged them, saying, "Be saved from this corrupt generation!" ⁴¹ So those who accepted his message were baptized, and that day about three thousand people were added to them.

A GENEROUS AND GROWING CHURCH

⁴² They devoted themselves to the apostles' teaching, to the fellowship, to the breaking of bread, and to prayer.

⁴³ Everyone was filled with awe, and many wonders and signs were being performed through the apostles.

⁴⁴ Now all the believers were together and held all things in common. ⁴⁵ They sold their possessions and property and distributed the proceeds to all, as any had need. ⁴⁶ Every day they devoted themselves to meeting together in the temple, and broke bread from house to house. They ate their food with joyful and sincere hearts, ⁴⁷ praising God and enjoying the favor of all the people. Every day the Lord added to their number those who were being saved.

SACRED SPACE

When Moses encountered the presence of God in the burning bush, God told the eighty-year-old shepherd, "Do not come closer…Remove the sandals from your feet, for the place where you are standing is holy ground" (Ex 3:5). Mount Sinai, where this scene took place, was made of the same rock and dirt as the other mountains in the region, but it was considered sacred because God's presence was there.

Throughout Scripture, God's presence turns ordinary land and ordinary buildings into holy places.

The Sacred Tabernacle and Temple

In the Old Testament, the temple and the tabernacle are the primary examples of sacred space.

Because these spaces were set apart for the glorious presence of the Lord, they were to be kept pure. That is why God told Moses, "You must keep the Israelites from their uncleanness, so that they do not die by defiling my tabernacle that is among them" (Lv 15:31).

This holiness is why the temple furnishings were crafted with the finest materials to exact specifications, and it's also why God prescribed that certain sacrifices be performed. For instance, on the Day of Atonement, blood was sprinkled to make "atonement for the most holy place, the tent of meeting, and the altar" to purify the sacred space itself from the uncleanness of the people (Lv 16:20).

Access to the tabernacle and the temple were restricted by degree, with more restrictions the closer one came to the Most Holy Place (Nm 18:22–23; 2Ch 23:6). Only the high priest was allowed to enter the Most Holy Place, and only then on the Day of Atonement (Lv 2:16–19).

The Sacred Land

Israel itself, the land of promise, was also set apart as holy.

Like the temple and the tabernacle, the land itself could be defiled by the disobedience of the people. That is why God commanded, "Do not make the land unclean where you live and where I dwell; for I, the Lord, reside among the Israelites" (Nm 35:34).

In the time of Elisha, the Aramean military commander Naaman recognized that the land of Israel was anything but ordinary because of the God who dwelled there. After being healed of his leprosy by the Lord, Namaan made a special request of the prophet: "Please let your servant be given as much soil as a pair of mules can carry, for your servant will no longer offer a burnt offering or a sacrifice to any other god but the Lord" (2Kg 5:17). Naaman wanted to stand on holy ground when he worshiped the God of Israel.

The Sacred People

In the New Testament, God fulfilled an amazing promise when He sent His Holy Spirit to live within His people. Sacred space is no longer confined to a certain nation or a certain spot on the map.

Because followers of Christ now carry the presence of God with them wherever they go, Christians are individually and collectively a temple of the Lord (1Co 3:16; 6:19–20). Followers of Jesus are now both temple-bearers and a royal priesthood (1Pt 2:9).

The Sacred World

The world will one day be redeemed from the curse of sin and death, and it will all be sacred—every last corner and molecule—as it was always intended to be.

At the end of history, heaven will come to earth, and the kingdom of this world will become the kingdom of God (Rv 11:15). On that day, "the earth shall be filled with the glory of the Lord" (Nm 14:21 ESV; Hab 2:14; Eph 4:10).

DAY 18

THE TEMPLE OF THE LIVING GOD

The people of God are the temple of God; His presence is active in the Church.

1 CORINTHIANS 3:9-17

⁹ For we are God's coworkers. You are God's field, God's building.

¹⁰ According to God's grace that was given to me, I have laid a foundation as a skilled master builder, and another builds on it. But each one is to be careful how he builds on it. ¹¹ For no one can lay any foundation other than what has been laid down. That foundation is Jesus Christ. ¹² If anyone builds on the foundation with gold, silver, costly stones, wood, hay, or straw, ¹³ each one's work will become obvious. For the day will disclose it, because it will be revealed by fire; the fire will test the quality of each one's work. ¹⁴ If anyone's work that he has built survives, he will receive a reward. ¹⁵ If anyone's work is burned up, he will experience loss, but he himself will be saved—but only as through fire.

¹⁶ Don't you yourselves know that you are God's temple and that the Spirit of God lives in you? ¹⁷ If anyone destroys God's temple, God will destroy him; for God's temple is holy, and that is what you are.

2 CORINTHIANS 6:16-18

¹⁶ And what agreement does the temple of God have with idols? For we are the temple of the living God, as God said:

> I will dwell
> and walk among them,
> and I will be their God,
> and they will be my people.
> ¹⁷ Therefore, come out from among them
> and be separate, says the Lord;
> do not touch any unclean thing,
> and I will welcome you.

¹⁸ And I will be a Father to you,
and you will be sons and daughters to me,
says the Lord Almighty.

NOTES

JOHN 4:20-24

²⁰ "Our ancestors worshiped on this mountain, but you Jews say that the place to worship is in Jerusalem."

²¹ Jesus told her, "Believe me, woman, an hour is coming when you will worship the Father neither on this mountain nor in Jerusalem. ²² You Samaritans worship what you do not know. We worship what we do know, because salvation is from the Jews. ²³ But an hour is coming, and is now here, when the true worshipers will worship the Father in Spirit and in truth. Yes, the Father wants such people to worship him. ²⁴ God is spirit, and those who worship him must worship in Spirit and in truth."

1 CHRONICLES 29:2

So to the best of my ability I've made provision for the house of my God: gold for the gold articles, silver for the silver, bronze for the bronze, iron for the iron, and wood for the wood, as well as onyx, stones for mounting, antimony, stones of various colors, all kinds of precious stones, and a great quantity of marble.

1 PETER 2:4-5

⁴ As you come to him, a living stone—rejected by people but chosen and honored by God— ⁵ you yourselves, as living stones, a spiritual house, are being built to be a holy priesthood to offer spiritual sacrifices acceptable to God through Jesus Christ.

EPHESIANS 2:19-22

¹⁹ So, then, you are no longer foreigners and strangers, but fellow citizens with the saints, and members of God's household, ²⁰ built on the foundation of the apostles and prophets, with Christ Jesus himself as the cornerstone. ²¹ In him the whole building, being put together, grows into a holy temple in the Lord. ²² In him you are also being built together for God's dwelling in the Spirit.

DAY 19

LIFE WITH GOD IN THE GARDEN CITY

One day, in the new heavens and new earth, God will dwell with His people as He did in the beginning.

ISAIAH 65:17–25

A NEW CREATION

17 "For I will create new heavens and a new earth;
the past events will not be remembered or come
    to mind.
18 Then be glad and rejoice forever
in what I am creating;
for I will create Jerusalem to be a joy
and its people to be a delight.
19 I will rejoice in Jerusalem
and be glad in my people.
The sound of weeping and crying
will no longer be heard in her.
20 In her, a nursing infant will no longer live
only a few days,
or an old man not live out his days.
Indeed, the one who dies at a hundred years old
will be mourned as a young man,
and the one who misses a hundred years
will be considered cursed.
21 People will build houses and live in them;
they will plant vineyards and eat their fruit.
22 They will not build and others live in them;
they will not plant and others eat.
For my people's lives will be
like the lifetime of a tree.
My chosen ones will fully enjoy
the work of their hands.
23 They will not labor without success
or bear children destined for disaster,
for they will be a people blessed by the Lord
along with their descendants.
24 Even before they call, I will answer;
while they are still speaking, I will hear.
25 The wolf and the lamb will feed together,
and the lion will eat straw like cattle,
but the serpent's food will be dust!
They will not do what is evil or destroy
on my entire holy mountain,"
says the Lord.

REVELATION 2:7

"Let anyone who has ears to hear listen to what the Spirit says to the churches. To the one who conquers, I will give the right to eat from the tree of life, which is in the paradise of God."

REVELATION 3:21

"To the one who conquers I will give the right to sit with me on my throne, just as I also conquered and sat down with my Father on his throne."

REVELATION 21:1-4, 22

THE NEW CREATION

¹ Then I saw a new heaven and a new earth; for the first heaven and the first earth had passed away, and the sea was no more. ² I also saw the holy city, the new Jerusalem, coming down out of heaven from God, prepared like a bride adorned for her husband.

³ Then I heard a loud voice from the throne: Look, God's dwelling is with humanity, and he will live with them. They will be his peoples, and God himself will be with them and will be their God. ⁴ He will wipe away every tear from their eyes. Death will be no more; grief, crying, and pain will be no more, because the previous things have passed away.

…

²² I did not see a temple in it, because the Lord God the Almighty and the Lamb are its temple.

REVELATION 22:1-5

THE SOURCE OF LIFE

¹ Then he showed me the river of the water of life, clear as crystal, flowing from the throne of God and of the Lamb ² down the middle of the city's main street. The tree of life was on each side of the river, bearing twelve kinds of fruit, producing its fruit every month. The leaves of the tree are for healing the nations, ³ and there will no longer be any curse. The throne of God and of the Lamb will be in the city, and his servants will worship him. ⁴ They will see his face, and his name will be on their foreheads. ⁵ Night will be no more; people will not need the light of a lamp or the light of the sun, because the Lord God will give them light, and they will reign forever and ever.

GRACE DAY

Take this day to catch up on your reading, pray, and rest in the presence of the Lord.

Night will be no more; people will not need the light of a lamp or the light of the sun, because the Lord God will give them light, and they will reign forever and ever.

REVELATION 22:5

DAY 20

DAY 21

WEEKLY

Scripture is God-breathed and true. When we memorize it, we carry the good news of Jesus with us wherever we go.

Over the course of this reading plan, we've worked on memorizing Psalm 73:28. This week, we will memorize the final line of the verse.

TRUTH

WEEK 3

BUT AS FOR ME, GOD'S PRESENCE IS MY GOOD.

I HAVE MADE THE LORD GOD MY REFUGE,

SO I CAN TELL ABOUT ALL YOU DO.

Psalm 73:28

SECTION 2

"Think often on God, by day, by night . . .
He is always near you and with you; leave
Him not alone."

BROTHER LAWRENCE

In response to what you've read and learned in Section 2 about the presence of God, take time to focus on His presence using one or more of the practices listed here. For tips and reminders about each one, refer back to pages 12–17. Use the space provided to journal about or reflect on your experience.

Make intentional time and space.
Meditate on God's Word.
Pray.
Worship.
Confess.

GOD'S DWELLING PLACE

Additional response sheets are included on pages 146–153.

RESPONSE

DATE

3

THE PROMISE OF GOD'S PRESENCE

> "And remember, I am with you always, to the end of the age."
>
> MATTHEW 28:20

God has always invited us to enter into His presence. Jesus called people to walk with Him as His disciples, and when He ascended to heaven, He promised His followers, "I am with you always" (Mt 28:20). With the knowledge that Christ's Spirit is always with us, we have access to true hope and peace as we wait for His return and a promised eternity in God's presence.

DAY 22

GOD PROMISES HIS PRESENCE

From the call of Abram to our inclusion as spiritual descendants, God's promises to His people are marked by His presence.

GENESIS 12:1–7

THE CALL OF ABRAM

¹ The Lord said to Abram:

> Go from your land,
> your relatives,
> and your father's house
> to the land that I will show you.
> ² I will make you into a great nation,
> I will bless you,
> I will make your name great,
> and you will be a blessing.
> ³ I will bless those who bless you,
> I will curse anyone who treats you
>   with contempt,
> and all the peoples on earth
> will be blessed through you.

⁴ So Abram went, as the Lord had told him, and Lot went with him. Abram was seventy-five years old when he left Haran. ⁵ He took his wife, Sarai, his nephew Lot, all the possessions they had accumulated, and the people they had acquired in Haran, and they set out for the land of Canaan. When they came to the land of Canaan, ⁶ Abram passed through the land to the site of Shechem, at the oak of Moreh. (At that time the Canaanites were in the land.) ⁷ The Lord appeared to Abram and said, "To your offspring I will give this land." So he built an altar there to the Lord who had appeared to him.

GENESIS 17:1–8

COVENANT CIRCUMCISION

¹ When Abram was ninety-nine years old, the Lord appeared to him, saying, "I am God Almighty. Live in my presence and be blameless. ² I will set up my covenant between me and you, and I will multiply you greatly."

³ Then Abram fell facedown and God spoke with him: ⁴ "As for me, here is my covenant with you: You will become the father of many nations. ⁵ Your name will no longer be Abram; your name will be Abraham, for I will make you the father of many nations. ⁶ I will make you extremely fruitful and will make nations and kings come from you. ⁷ I will confirm my covenant that is between me and you and your future offspring throughout their generations. It is a permanent covenant to be your God and the God of your offspring after you. ⁸ And to you and your future offspring I will give the land where you are residing—all the land of Canaan—as a permanent possession, and I will be their God."

GENESIS 26:1-6, 23-24

THE PROMISE REAFFIRMED TO ISAAC

¹ There was another famine in the land in addition to the one that had occurred in Abraham's time. And Isaac went to Abimelech, king of the Philistines, at Gerar. ² The LORD appeared to him and said, "Do not go down to Egypt. Live in the land that I tell you about; ³ stay in this land as an alien, and I will be with you and bless you. For I will give all these lands to you and your offspring, and I will confirm the oath that I swore to your father Abraham. ⁴ I will make your offspring as numerous as the stars of the sky, I will give your offspring all these lands, and all the nations of the earth will be blessed by your offspring, ⁵ because Abraham listened to me and kept my mandate, my commands, my statutes, and my instructions." ⁶ So Isaac settled in Gerar.

...

THE LORD APPEARS TO ISAAC

²³ From there he went up to Beer-sheba, ²⁴ and the LORD appeared to him that night and said, "I am the God of your father Abraham. Do not be afraid, for I am with you. I will bless you and multiply your offspring because of my servant Abraham."

GENESIS 28:10-22

JACOB AT BETHEL

¹⁰ Jacob left Beer-sheba and went toward Haran. ¹¹ He reached a certain place and spent the night there because the sun had set. He took one of the stones from the place, put it there at his head, and lay down in that place. ¹² And he dreamed: A stairway was set on the ground with its top

reaching the sky, and God's angels were going up and down on it. ¹³ The LORD was standing there beside him, saying, "I am the LORD, the God of your father Abraham and the God of Isaac. I will give you and your offspring the land on which you are lying. ¹⁴ Your offspring will be like the dust of the earth, and you will spread out toward the west, the east, the north, and the south. All the peoples on earth will be blessed through you and your offspring. ¹⁵ Look, I am with you and will watch over you wherever you go. I will bring you back to this land, for I will not leave you until I have done what I have promised you."

¹⁶ When Jacob awoke from his sleep, he said, "Surely the LORD is in this place, and I did not know it." ¹⁷ He was afraid and said, "What an awesome place this is! This is none other than the house of God. This is the gate of heaven."

¹⁸ Early in the morning Jacob took the stone that was near his head and set it up as a marker. He poured oil on top of it ¹⁹ and named the place Bethel, though previously the city was named Luz. ²⁰ Then Jacob made a vow: "If God will be with me and watch over me during this journey I'm making, if he provides me with food to eat and clothing to wear, ²¹ and if I return safely to my father's family, then the LORD will be my God. ²² This stone that I have set up as a marker will be God's house, and I will give to you a tenth of all that you give me."

GENESIS 32:24-30

JACOB WRESTLES WITH GOD

²⁴ Jacob was left alone, and a man wrestled with him until daybreak. ²⁵ When the man saw that he could not defeat him, he struck Jacob's hip socket as they wrestled and dislocated his hip. ²⁶ Then he said to Jacob, "Let me go, for it is daybreak."

But Jacob said, "I will not let you go unless you bless me."

²⁷ "What is your name?" the man asked.

"Jacob," he replied.

²⁸ "Your name will no longer be Jacob," he said. "It will be Israel because you have struggled with God and with men and have prevailed."

²⁹ Then Jacob asked him, "Please tell me your name."

But he answered, "Why do you ask my name?" And he blessed him there.

³⁰ Jacob then named the place Peniel, "For I have seen God face to face," he said, "yet my life has been spared."

GENESIS 35:9-12

⁹ God appeared to Jacob again after he returned from Paddan-aram, and he blessed him. ¹⁰ God said to him, "Your name is Jacob; you will no longer be named Jacob, but your name will be Israel." So he named him Israel. ¹¹ God also said to him, "I am God Almighty. Be fruitful and multiply. A nation, indeed an assembly of nations, will come from you, and kings will descend from you. ¹² I will give to you the land that I gave to Abraham and Isaac. And I will give the land to your future descendants."

ACTS 3:25

You are the sons of the prophets and of the covenant that God made with your ancestors, saying to Abraham, And all the families of the earth will be blessed through your offspring.

DAY 23

GOD'S PRESENCE EQUIPS US

God calls His people to take part in establishing His kingdom on earth, and He equips us by going with us.

JOSHUA 1:1–9, 17

ENCOURAGEMENT OF JOSHUA

¹ After the death of Moses the Lord's servant, the Lord spoke to Joshua son of Nun, Moses's assistant: ² "Moses my servant is dead. Now you and all the people prepare to cross over the Jordan to the land I am giving the Israelites. ³ I have given you every place where the sole of your foot treads, just as I promised Moses. ⁴ Your territory will be from the wilderness and Lebanon to the great river, the Euphrates River—all the land of the Hittites—and west to the Mediterranean Sea. ⁵ No one will be able to stand against you as long as you live. I will be with you, just as I was with Moses. I will not leave you or abandon you.

⁶ "Be strong and courageous, for you will distribute the land I swore to their ancestors to give them as an inheritance. ⁷ Above all, be strong and very courageous to observe carefully the whole instruction my servant Moses commanded you. Do not turn from it to the right or the left, so that you will have success wherever you go. ⁸ This book of instruction must not depart from your mouth; you are to meditate on it day and night so that you may carefully observe everything written in it. For then you will prosper and succeed in whatever you do. ⁹ Haven't I commanded you: be strong and courageous? Do not be afraid or discouraged, for the Lord your God is with you wherever you go."

...

¹⁷ We will obey you, just as we obeyed Moses in everything. Certainly the Lord your God will be with you, as he was with Moses.

JOSHUA 10:8–14

⁸ The Lord said to Joshua, "Do not be afraid of them, for I have handed them over to you. Not one of them will be able to stand against you."

⁹ So Joshua caught them by surprise, after marching all night from Gilgal. ¹⁰ The Lord threw them into confusion before Israel. He defeated them in a great slaughter at Gibeon, chased them through the ascent of Beth-horon, and struck them down as far as Azekah and Makkedah. ¹¹ As they fled before Israel, the Lord threw large hailstones on them from the sky along the descent of Beth-horon all the way to Azekah, and they died. More of them died from the hail than the Israelites killed with the sword.

NOTES

NOTES

¹² On the day the Lord gave the Amorites over to the Israelites, Joshua spoke to the Lord in the presence of Israel:

> "Sun, stand still over Gibeon,
> and moon, over the Valley of Aijalon."
> ¹³ And the sun stood still
> and the moon stopped
> until the nation took vengeance on its enemies.

Isn't this written in the Book of Jashar?

> So the sun stopped
> in the middle of the sky
> and delayed its setting
> almost a full day.

¹⁴ There has been no day like it before or since, when the Lord listened to a man, because the Lord fought for Israel.

ROMANS 8:31-39

THE BELIEVER'S TRIUMPH

³¹ What, then, are we to say about these things? If God is for us, who is against us? ³² He did not even spare his own Son but gave him up for us all. How will he not also with him grant us everything? ³³ Who can bring an accusation against God's elect? God is the one who justifies. ³⁴ Who is the one who condemns? Christ Jesus is the one who died, but even more, has been raised; he also is at the right hand of God and intercedes for us. ³⁵ Who can separate us from the love of Christ? Can affliction or distress or persecution or famine or nakedness or danger or sword? ³⁶ As it is written:

> Because of you
> we are being put to death all day long;
> we are counted as sheep to be slaughtered.

³⁷ No, in all these things we are more than conquerors through him who loved us. ³⁸ For I am persuaded that neither death nor life, nor angels nor rulers, nor things present nor things to come, nor powers, ³⁹ nor height nor depth, nor any other created thing will be able to separate us from the love of God that is in Christ Jesus our Lord.

NOTES

DATE

DAY 24

WALKING IN GOD'S PRESENCE

We are called to follow Jesus and walk with Him daily, learning about life in His kingdom.

GENESIS 5:21-24

²¹ Enoch was 65 years old when he fathered Methuselah. ²² And after he fathered Methuselah, Enoch walked with God 300 years and fathered other sons and daughters. ²³ So Enoch's life lasted 365 years. ²⁴ Enoch walked with God; then he was not there because God took him.

MATTHEW 4:18-25

THE FIRST DISCIPLES

¹⁸ As he was walking along the Sea of Galilee, he saw two brothers, Simon (who is called Peter), and his brother Andrew. They were casting a net into the sea—for they were fishermen. ¹⁹ "Follow me," he told them, "and I will make you fish for people." ²⁰ Immediately they left their nets and followed him.

²¹ Going on from there, he saw two other brothers, James the son of Zebedee, and his brother John. They were in a boat with Zebedee their father, preparing their nets, and he called them. ²² Immediately they left the boat and their father and followed him.

TEACHING, PREACHING, AND HEALING

²³ Now Jesus began to go all over Galilee, teaching in their synagogues, preaching the good news of the kingdom, and healing every disease and sickness among the people. ²⁴ Then the news about him spread throughout Syria. So they brought to him all those who were afflicted, those suffering from various diseases and intense pains, the demon-possessed, the epileptics, and the paralytics. And he healed them. ²⁵ Large crowds followed him from Galilee, the Decapolis, Jerusalem, Judea, and beyond the Jordan.

LUKE 8:1-3

MANY WOMEN SUPPORT CHRIST'S WORK

¹ Afterward he was traveling from one town and village to another, preaching and telling the good news of the kingdom of God. The Twelve were with him, ² and also some women who had been healed of evil spirits and sicknesses: Mary, called Magdalene (seven demons had come out of her); ³ Joanna the wife of Chuza, Herod's steward; Susanna; and many others who were supporting them from their possessions.

NOTES

LUKE 10:38–42

MARTHA AND MARY

[38] While they were traveling, he entered a village, and a woman named Martha welcomed him into her home. [39] She had a sister named Mary, who also sat at the Lord's feet and was listening to what he said. [40] But Martha was distracted by her many tasks, and she came up and asked, "Lord, don't you care that my sister has left me to serve alone? So tell her to give me a hand."

[41] The Lord answered her, "Martha, Martha, you are worried and upset about many things, [42] but one thing is necessary. Mary has made the right choice, and it will not be taken away from her."

MARK 8:34–38

TAKE UP YOUR CROSS

[34] Calling the crowd along with his disciples, he said to them, "If anyone wants to follow after me, let him deny himself, take up his cross, and follow me.

[35] For whoever wants to save his life will lose it, but whoever loses his life because of me and the gospel will save it.

[36] For what does it benefit someone to gain the whole world and yet lose his life? [37] What can anyone give in exchange for his life? [38] For whoever is ashamed of me and my words in this adulterous and sinful generation, the Son of Man will also be ashamed of him when he comes in the glory of his Father with the holy angels."

JOHN 15:1–8

THE VINE AND THE BRANCHES

[1] "I am the true vine, and my Father is the gardener. [2] Every branch in me that does not produce fruit he removes, and he prunes every branch that produces fruit so that it will produce more fruit. [3] You are already clean because of the word I have spoken to you. [4] Remain in me, and I in you. Just as a branch is unable to produce fruit by itself unless it remains on the vine, neither can you unless you remain in me. [5] I am the vine;

you are the branches. The one who remains in me and I in him produces much fruit, because you can do nothing without me. ⁶ If anyone does not remain in me, he is thrown aside like a branch and he withers. They gather them, throw them into the fire, and they are burned. ⁷ If you remain in me and my words remain in you, ask whatever you want and it will be done for you. ⁸ My Father is glorified by this: that you produce much fruit and prove to be my disciples."

GALATIANS 5:16–26

THE SPIRIT VERSUS THE FLESH

¹⁶ I say, then, walk by the Spirit and you will certainly not carry out the desire of the flesh. ¹⁷ For the flesh desires what is against the Spirit, and the Spirit desires what is against the flesh; these are opposed to each other, so that you don't do what you want. ¹⁸ But if you are led by the Spirit, you are not under the law.

¹⁹ Now the works of the flesh are obvious: sexual immorality, moral impurity, promiscuity, ²⁰ idolatry, sorcery, hatreds, strife, jealousy, outbursts of anger, selfish ambitions, dissensions, factions, ²¹ envy, drunkenness, carousing, and anything similar. I am warning you about these things—as I warned you before—that those who practice such things will not inherit the kingdom of God.

²² But the fruit of the Spirit is love, joy, peace, patience, kindness, goodness, faithfulness, ²³ gentleness, and self-control. The law is not against such things. ²⁴ Now those who belong to Christ Jesus have crucified the flesh with its passions and desires. ²⁵ If we live by the Spirit, let us also keep in step with the Spirit. ²⁶ Let us not become conceited, provoking one another, envying one another.

PSALMS, WORSHIP, and the PRESENCE of GOD

For thousands of years, God's people have read and sung the psalms as a means of seeking, celebrating, lamenting, and resting in God's presence. Today, the psalms still serve as an invitation to reflect on the presence of God in every circumstance and season.

———

As you read the examples below, consider incorporating the following psalms into your time practicing God's presence, exploring and praying through psalms as a way to worship the Lord and enjoy the peace of His presence.

**PSALMS ENCOURAGE US
TO SEEK GOD'S PRESENCE.**

SEEK

Instead of turning away from God during trials, we can find deeper intimacy with Him when we seek Him with our whole hearts.

PSALM 63:1-5

God, you are my God; I eagerly seek you.
I thirst for you;
my body faints for you
in a land that is dry, desolate, and without water.
So I gaze on you in the sanctuary
to see your strength and your glory.

My lips will glorify you
because your faithful love is better than life.
So I will bless you as long as I live;
at your name, I will lift up my hands.
You satisfy me as with rich food;
my mouth will praise you with joyful lips.

See also Psalm 86

**PSALMS PROVIDE SPACE FOR
US TO REST IN GOD'S PRESENCE.**

REST

God's presence is a shelter for our weary hearts. We can experience peace and calm when we quiet ourselves before Him.

PSALM 91:1-4, 9-10

The one who lives under the protection
of the Most High
dwells in the shadow of the Almighty.

I will say concerning the Lord, who is my
refuge and my fortress,
my God in whom I trust:
He himself will rescue you from the bird trap,
from the destructive plague.
He will cover you with his feathers;
you will take refuge under his wings.
His faithfulness will be a protective shield.

. . .

Because you have made the Lord—my refuge,
the Most High—your dwelling place,
no harm will come to you;
no plague will come near your tent.

See also Psalm 16

PSALMS OFFER LANGUAGE FOR US
TO MOURN WHAT FEELS LIKE THE
LOSS OF GOD'S PRESENCE.

LAMENT

In Christ, we cannot be separated from God's
love and presence. Even when He feels far,
we can trust that He is always near.

PSALM 88:13-18

But I call to you for help, LORD;
in the morning my prayer meets you.
LORD, why do you reject me?
Why do you hide your face from me?
From my youth,
I have been suffering and near death.
I suffer your horrors; I am desperate.
Your wrath sweeps over me;
your terrors destroy me.
They surround me like water all day long;
they close in on me from every side.
You have distanced loved one and neighbor
from me;
darkness is my only friend.

See also Psalm 42

PSALMS CALL US TO PRAISE GOD FOR
THE EVIDENCE OF HIS PRESENCE.

CELEBRATE

When we remember God's power and nearness, it is good to celebrate Him with music, worship, and shouts of praise.

PSALM 95:1–7

Come, let's shout joyfully to the LORD,
shout triumphantly to the rock of our salvation!
Let's enter his presence with thanksgiving;
let's shout triumphantly to him in song.

For the LORD is a great God,
a great King above all gods.
The depths of the earth are in his hand,
and the mountain peaks are his.
The sea is his; he made it.
His hands formed the dry land.

Come, let's worship and bow down;
let's kneel before the LORD our Maker.
For he is our God,
and we are the people of his pasture,
the sheep under his care.

See also Psalm 146

MATTHEW 28:16-20

THE GREAT COMMISSION

¹⁶ The eleven disciples traveled to Galilee, to the mountain where Jesus had directed them. ¹⁷ When they saw him, they worshiped, but some doubted. ¹⁸ Jesus came near and said to them, "All authority has been given to me in heaven and on earth. ¹⁹ Go, therefore, and make disciples of all nations, baptizing them in the name of the Father and of the Son and of the Holy Spirit, ²⁰ teaching them to observe everything I have commanded you. And remember, I am with you always, to the end of the age."

JOHN 14:15-31

ANOTHER COUNSELOR PROMISED

¹⁵ "If you love me, you will keep my commands. ¹⁶ And I will ask the Father, and he will give you another Counselor to be with you forever. ¹⁷ He is the Spirit of truth. The world is unable to receive him because it doesn't see him or know him. But you do know him, because he remains with you and will be in you.

THE FATHER, THE SON, AND THE HOLY SPIRIT

¹⁸ "I will not leave you as orphans; I am coming to you. ¹⁹ In a little while the world will no longer see me, but you will see me. Because I live, you will live too. ²⁰ On that day you will know that I am in my Father, you are in me, and I am in you. ²¹ The one who has my commands and keeps them is the one who loves me. And the one who loves me will be loved by my Father. I also will love him and will reveal myself to him."

²² Judas (not Iscariot) said to him, "Lord, how is it you're going to reveal yourself to us and not to the world?"

²³ Jesus answered, "If anyone loves me, he will keep my word. My Father will love him, and we will come to him and make our home with him. ²⁴ The one who doesn't love me will not keep my words. The word that you hear is not mine but is from the Father who sent me.

²⁵ "I have spoken these things to you while I remain with you. ²⁶ But the Counselor, the Holy Spirit, whom the Father will send in my name, will teach you all things and remind you of everything I have told you.

NOTES

JESUS'S GIFT OF PEACE

²⁷ "Peace I leave with you. My peace I give to you. I do not give to you as the world gives. Don't let your heart be troubled or fearful. ²⁸ You have heard me tell you, 'I am going away and I am coming to you.' If you loved me, you would rejoice that I am going to the Father, because the Father is greater than I. ²⁹ I have told you now before it happens so that when it does happen you may believe. ³⁰ I will not talk with you much longer, because the ruler of the world is coming. He has no power over me. ³¹ On the contrary, so that the world may know that I love the Father, I do as the Father commanded me.

"Get up; let's leave this place."

JOHN 15:1-8, 26

THE VINE AND THE BRANCHES

¹ "I am the true vine, and my Father is the gardener. ² Every branch in me that does not produce fruit he removes, and he prunes every branch that produces fruit so that it will produce more fruit. ³ You are already clean because of the word I have spoken to you. ⁴ Remain in me, and I in you. Just as a branch is unable to produce fruit by itself unless it remains on the vine, neither can you unless you remain in me. ⁵ I am the vine; you are the branches. The one who remains in me and I in him produces much fruit, because you can do nothing without me. ⁶ If anyone does not remain in me, he is thrown aside like a branch and he withers. They gather them, throw them into the fire, and they are burned. ⁷ If you remain in me and my words remain in you, ask whatever you want and it will be done for you. ⁸ My Father is glorified by this: that you produce much fruit and prove to be my disciples.

. . .

THE COUNSELOR'S MINISTRY

²⁶ "When the Counselor comes, the one I will send to you from the Father —the Spirit of truth who proceeds from the Father—he will testify about me."

JOHN 16:13-15

¹³ "When the Spirit of truth comes, he will guide you into all the truth. For he will not speak on his own, but he will speak whatever he hears. He

will also declare to you what is to come. ¹⁴ He will glorify me, because he will take from what is mine and declare it to you. ¹⁵ Everything the Father has is mine. This is why I told you that he takes from what is mine and will declare it to you."

JOHN 20:19–21

THE DISCIPLES COMMISSIONED

¹⁹ When it was evening on that first day of the week, the disciples were gathered together with the doors locked because they feared the Jews. Jesus came, stood among them, and said to them, "Peace be with you."

²⁰ Having said this, he showed them his hands and his side. So the disciples rejoiced when they saw the Lord.

²¹ Jesus said to them again, "Peace be with you. As the Father has sent me, I also send you."

1 JOHN 3:24

The one who keeps his commands remains in him, and he in him. And the way we know that he remains in us is from the Spirit he has given us.

EPHESIANS 1:13–14

¹³ In him you also were sealed with the promised Holy Spirit when you heard the word of truth, the gospel of your salvation, and when you believed.

¹⁴ The Holy Spirit is the down payment of our inheritance, until the redemption of the possession, to the praise of his glory.

DAY 26

ETERNITY IN GOD'S PRESENCE

In Christ, our place in God's presence is secure. We cannot be separated from His love.

JOHN 10:1–30

THE GOOD SHEPHERD

¹ "Truly I tell you, anyone who doesn't enter the sheep pen by the gate but climbs in some other way is a thief and a robber. ² The one who enters by the gate is the shepherd of the sheep. ³ The gatekeeper opens it for him, and the sheep hear his voice. He calls his own sheep by name and leads them out. ⁴ When he has brought all his own outside, he goes ahead of them. The sheep follow him because they know his voice. ⁵ They will never follow a stranger; instead they will run away from him, because they don't know the voice of strangers." ⁶ Jesus gave them this figure of speech, but they did not understand what he was telling them.

⁷ Jesus said again, "Truly I tell you, I am the gate for the sheep. ⁸ All who came before me are thieves and robbers, but the sheep didn't listen to them. ⁹ I am the gate. If anyone enters by me, he will be saved and will come in and go out and find pasture. ¹⁰ A thief comes only to steal and kill and destroy. I have come so that they may have life and have it in abundance.

¹¹ "I am the good shepherd. The good shepherd lays down his life for the sheep. ¹² The hired hand, since he is not the shepherd and doesn't own the sheep, leaves them and runs away when he sees a wolf coming. The wolf then snatches and scatters them. ¹³ This happens because he is a hired hand and doesn't care about the sheep.

¹⁴ "I am the good shepherd. I know my own, and my own know me, ¹⁵ just as the Father knows me, and I know the Father. I lay down my life for the sheep. ¹⁶ But I have other sheep that are not from this sheep pen; I must bring them also, and they will listen to my voice. Then there will be one flock, one shepherd. ¹⁷ This is why the Father loves me, because I lay down my life so that I may take it up again. ¹⁸ No one takes it from me, but I lay it down on my own. I have the right to lay it down, and I have the right to take it up again. I have received this command from my Father."

¹⁹ Again the Jews were divided because of these words. ²⁰ Many of them were saying, "He has a demon and he's crazy. Why do you listen to him?" ²¹ Others were saying, "These aren't the words of someone who is demon-possessed. Can a demon open the eyes of the blind?"

NOTES

JESUS AT THE FESTIVAL OF DEDICATION

[22] Then the Festival of Dedication took place in Jerusalem, and it was winter. [23] Jesus was walking in the temple in Solomon's Colonnade. [24] The Jews surrounded him and asked, "How long are you going to keep us in suspense? If you are the Messiah, tell us plainly."

[25] "I did tell you and you don't believe," Jesus answered them. "The works that I do in my Father's name testify about me. [26] But you don't believe because you are not of my sheep. [27] My sheep hear my voice, I know them, and they follow me. [28] I give them eternal life, and they will never perish. No one will snatch them out of my hand. [29] My Father, who has given them to me, is greater than all. No one is able to snatch them out of the Father's hand. [30] I and the Father are one."

JOHN 14:1–3

THE WAY TO THE FATHER

[1] "Don't let your heart be troubled. Believe in God; believe also in me. [2] In my Father's house are many rooms. If it were not so, would I have told you that I am going to prepare a place for you? [3] If I go away and prepare a place for you, I will come again and take you to myself, so that where I am you may be also."

LUKE 23:32–43

CRUCIFIED BETWEEN TWO CRIMINALS

[32] Two others—criminals—were also led away to be executed with him. [33] When they arrived at the place called The Skull, they crucified him there, along with the criminals, one on the right and one on the left. [34] Then Jesus said, "Father, forgive them, because they do not know what they are doing." And they divided his clothes and cast lots.

[35] The people stood watching, and even the leaders were scoffing: "He saved others; let him save himself if this is God's Messiah, the Chosen One!" [36] The soldiers also mocked him. They came offering him sour wine [37] and said, "If you are the king of the Jews, save yourself!"

[38] An inscription was above him: THIS IS THE KING OF THE JEWS.

⁶⁹ Then one of the criminals hanging there began to yell insults at him: "Aren't you the Messiah? Save yourself and us!"

⁴⁰ But the other answered, rebuking him: "Don't you even fear God, since you are undergoing the same punishment? ⁴¹ We are punished justly, because we're getting back what we deserve for the things we did, but this man has done nothing wrong." ⁴² Then he said, "Jesus, remember me when you come into your kingdom."

⁴³ And he said to him, "Truly I tell you, today you will be with me in paradise."

ROMANS 6:23

For the wages of sin is death, but the gift of God is eternal life in Christ Jesus our Lord.

ROMANS 14:8

If we live, we live for the Lord; and if we die, we die for the Lord. Therefore, whether we live or die, we belong to the Lord.

1 THESSALONIANS 4:16-17

¹⁶ For the Lord himself will descend from heaven with a shout, with the archangel's voice, and with the trumpet of God, and the dead in Christ will rise first. ¹⁷ Then we who are still alive, who are left, will be caught up together with them in the clouds to meet the Lord in the air, and so we will always be with the Lord.

GRACE DAY

Take this day to catch up on your reading, pray, and rest in the presence of the Lord.

The LORD is my strength and my song; he has become my salvation. This is my God, and I will praise him, my father's God, and I will exalt him.

EXODUS 15:2

DAY 27

DAY 28

WEEKLY

Scripture is God-breathed and true. When we memorize it, we carry the good news of Jesus with us wherever we go.

Throughout this reading plan, we've memorized Psalm 73:28. Take time this week to recite the entire verse at once, and practice your memorization by copying it in the space provided.

TRUTH

WEEK 4

BUT AS FOR ME, GOD'S PRESENCE IS MY GOOD.
I HAVE MADE THE LORD GOD MY REFUGE,
SO I CAN TELL ABOUT ALL YOU DO.

Psalm 73:28

SECTION 3

THE PROMISE OF GOD'S PRESENCE

"There is not in the world a kind of life more sweet and delightful than that of a continual conversation with God."

BROTHER LAWRENCE

In response to what you've read and learned in Section 3 about the presence of God, take time to focus on His presence using one or more of the practices listed here. For tips and reminders about each one, refer back to pages 12-17. Use the space provided to journal about or reflect on your experience.

Make intentional time and space.
Meditate on God's Word.
Pray.
Worship.
Confess.

Additional response sheets are included on pages 146-153.

RESPONSE

DATE

BENEDICTION

"MAY THE LORD BLESS YOU AND PROTECT YOU; MAY THE LORD MAKE HIS FACE SHINE ON YOU AND BE GRACIOUS TO YOU; MAY THE LORD LOOK WITH FAVOR ON YOU AND GIVE YOU PEACE."

NUMBERS 6:24-26

PRACTICING THE PRESENCE OF GOD

Take time to focus on God's presence using one or more of the practices listed here. For tips and reminders about each one, refer back to pages 12–17. Use the space provided to journal about or reflect on your experience.

Make intentional time and space.
Meditate on God's Word.
Pray.
Worship.
Confess.

RESPONSE

DATE

PRACTICING THE PRESENCE OF GOD

Take time to focus on God's presence using one or more of the practices listed here. For tips and reminders about each one, refer back to pages 12-17. Use the space provided to journal about or reflect on your experience.

Make intentional time and space.
Meditate on God's Word.
Pray.
Worship.
Confess.

RESPONSE

DATE

PRACTICING THE PRESENCE OF GOD

Take time to focus on God's presence using one or more of the practices listed here. For tips and reminders about each one, refer back to pages 12-17. Use the space provided to journal about or reflect on your experience.

Make intentional time and space.
Meditate on God's Word.
Pray.
Worship.
Confess.

PRACTICING THE PRESENCE OF GOD

Take time to focus on God's presence using one or more of the practices listed here. For tips and reminders about each one, refer back to pages 12–17. Use the space provided to journal about or reflect on your experience.

Make intentional time and space.
Meditate on God's Word.
Pray.
Worship.
Confess.

DOWNLOAD THE APP

VISIT
hereadstruth.com

SHOP
shophereadstruth.com

CONTACT
hello@hereadstruth.com

CONNECT
#HeReadsTruth

LISTEN
She Reads Truth Podcast

CSB BOOK ABBREVIATIONS

OLD TESTAMENT
Genesis – Gn
Exodus – Ex
Leviticus – Lv
Numbers – Nm
Deuteronomy – Dt
Joshua – Jos
Judges – Jdg
Ruth – Ru
1 Samuel – 1Sm
2 Samuel – 2Sm
1 Kings – 1Kg
2 Kings – 2Kg
1 Chronicles – 1Ch
2 Chronicles – 2Ch
Ezra – Ezr
Nehemiah – Neh
Esther – Est
Job – Jb
Psalms – Ps
Proverbs – Pr
Ecclesiastes – Ec
Song of Solomon – Sg

Isaiah – Is
Jeremiah – Jr
Lamentations – Lm
Ezekiel – Ezk
Daniel – Dn
Hosea – Hs
Joel – Jl
Amos – Am
Obadiah – Ob
Jonah – Jnh
Micah – Mc
Nahum – Nah
Habakkuk – Hab
Zephaniah – Zph
Haggai – Hg
Zechariah – Zch
Malachi – Mal

NEW TESTAMENT
Matthew – Mt
Mark – Mk
Luke – Lk
John – Jn

Acts – Ac
Romans – Rm
1 Corinthians – 1Co
2 Corinthians – 2Co
Galatians – Gl
Ephesians – Eph
Philippians – Php
Colossians – Col
1 Thessalonians – 1Th
2 Thessalonians – 2Th
1 Timothy – 1Tm
2 Timothy – 2Tm
Titus – Ti
Philemon – Phm
Hebrews – Heb
James – Jms
1 Peter – 1Pt
2 Peter – 2Pt
1 John – 1Jn
2 John – 2Jn
3 John – 3Jn
Jude – Jd
Revelation – Rv

BIBLIOGRAPHY

Beale, G. K. *The Temple and the Church's Mission: A Biblical Theology of the Dwelling Place of God*. United Kingdom: InterVarsity Press, 2014.

Brother Lawrence. *The Practice of the Presence of God: Being Conversations and Letters of Nicholas Herman of Lorraine*. New York: Fleming H. Revell Company, 1895.

Hays, J. Daniel, and J. Scott Duvall. *God's Relational Presence: The Cohesive Center of Biblical Theology*. United States: Baker Publishing Group, 2019.

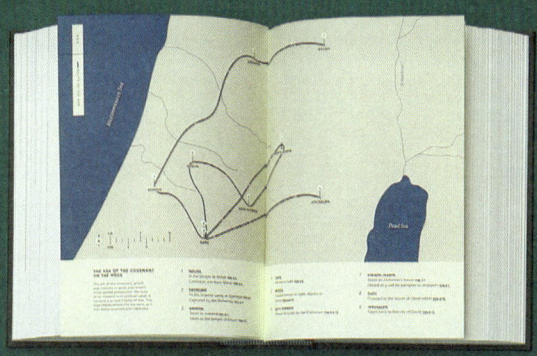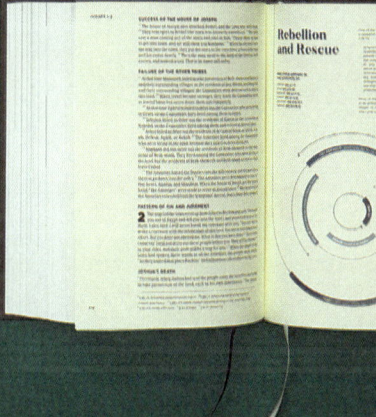

HE READS TRUTH | BIBLE

The *He Reads Truth Bible* includes a robust selection of thoughtfully-crafted theological extras to draw the reader back to Scripture and foster a growing affection for God and His Word.

Featuring the Christian Standard Bible (CSB) text, the *He Reads Truth Bible* maintains accuracy without sacrificing readability, making it easier to engage with Scripture's life-changing message and share it with others.

USE CODE HRTB15 FOR 15% OFF YOUR NEW HE READS TRUTH BIBLE

SHOPHEREADSTRUTH.COM

FOR THE RECORD

Where did I study?

- ☐ HOME
- ☐ OFFICE
- ☐ CHURCH
- ☐ SCHOOL
- ☐ COFFEE SHOP
- ☐ OTHER:

_____

_____

What was I listening to?

SONG: _____

ARTIST: _____

ALBUM: _____

_____

What time of day did I study?

- ☐ MORNING
- ☐ AFTERNOON
- ☐ NIGHT

_____

_____

What was happening in the world?

_____

_____

_____

_____

What was happening in my life?

_____

_____

_____

_____

_____

How did I find delight in God's Word?

_____

END DATE

_____ / _____ / _____